LANGUAGE ARTS

WILLIAM & MARY

THE CENTER FOR GIFTED EDUCATION

# The Pursuit of Justice

**Second Edition**

## Student Guide

Grades 7-8

Cover image © 2015 Shutterstock, Inc.

**Kendall Hunt**
publishing company

www.kendallhunt.com
*Send all inquiries to:*
4050 Westmark Drive
Dubuque, IA 52004-6657
1-800-542-6657

The College of William & Mary
School of Education
Center for Gifted Education
PO Box 8795
Williamsburg, VA 23187-8795
757-221-2362
www.cfge.wm.edu

Copyright © 2015 by Center for Gifted Education

ISBN 978-1-4652-5336-1

Kendall Hunt Publishing Company has the exclusive rights to reproduce this work, to prepare derivative works from this work, to publicly distribute this work, to publicly perform this work and to publicly display this work.

All rights reserved. No part of this publication may be reproduced, stored in a retrieval system, or transmitted, in any form or by any means, electronic, mechanical, photocopying, recording, or otherwise, without the prior written permission of Kendall Hunt Publishing Company.

Printed by: Lightning Source
United States of America
Batch number: 435336

Printed in the United States of America

# Contents



Copyright © Kendall Hunt Publishing Company

Copyright © Kendall Hunt Publishing Company

Copyright © Kendall Hunt Publishing Company

Copyright © Kendall Hunt Publishing Company

# Acknowledgments

**Teacher Developer**

Mary Ann Yedinak

**Center for Gifted Education Staff**

Dr. Tracy L. Cross, *Executive Director*

Dr. Kimberley L. Chandler, *Curriculum Director*

Pamela N. Harris, *Editorial Assistant*

Copyright © Kendall Hunt Publishing Company

# Letter to Student

Dear Student:

Perhaps you have noticed that life has moments when justice is served and times when life seems unfair. Have you ever thought about why sometimes life seems fair and balanced only to have a sense of disequilibrium strike, making you question the injustice that suddenly seems to be all around? You are about to begin a special language arts unit called *The Pursuit of Justice*. The unit is designed especially for students who have a high ability for delving into literature and making connections to society and life. The goals of the unit are as follows:

- To develop analytical and interpretive skills in literature and texts.
- To develop persuasive, argumentative, creative, and expository writing skills.
- To develop linguistic competency.
- To develop listening and oral communication skills.
- To develop reasoning skills.
- To develop an understanding of the concept of justice.

During this unit, you will consider the connections among people, historical events, popular culture, and yourself with regard to justice. This unit examines how justice and injustice shape people and the world. You will examine novels, short stories, poetry, art, and music throughout this unit. In addition, you will have ample opportunities for reading, writing, listening, and speaking. As you read the literature and texts, you will respond by thinking critically about them by analyzing ideas, structure, comparisons, vocabulary, and reasoning. Since *justice* is the overarching concept, insights regarding this concept will be ongoing.

Some activities in the unit will require you to work outside of class:

- Independent investigation on selected issues.
- Research on a significant issue in preparation for a written and oral presentation.

Copyright © Kendall Hunt Publishing Company

- Long term reading assignments:
  - *Of Mice and Men*
  - *No Promises in the Wind*
  - *To Kill a Mockingbird*
  - *Warriors Don't Cry*
  - *The Night Thoreau Spent in Jail*

The purpose of this book is to provide you with additional materials that you will need to participate in the unit. This student book contains poems, short stories, and Activity Pages related to the selection of readings.

The more tools a learner has at his or her disposal, the more opportunities an individual has to excel. During this unit, you will examine and learn to use many models to help organize your thinking. They include:

- The Concept Model
- The Literature Model
- The Vocabulary Model
- The Writing Process Model
- The Hamburger and Dagwood Models for Persuasive Writing
- The Reasoning Model
- The Research Model

Consider how Theodore Roosevelt said, "No man is above the law and no man below it." Let's seek ways to celebrate and pursue justice.

Sincerely,

*The Curriculum Development Team*
*The Center for Gifted Education at The College of William & Mary*

Copyright © Kendall Hunt Publishing Company

# Glossary of Literary Terms

**Allegory:** a narrative in which a literal meaning corresponds closely to a symbolic meaning and a lesson or moral is taught.

**Allusion:** an author's reference to a person, place, event, or piece of literature, which she expects her audience to recognize or understand.

**Anaphora:** the repetition of a word or phrase at the very beginning of successive phrases, clauses, or sentences.

**Character:** a person portrayed in a piece of literature with artistic license; a character is usually central to novels, short stories, and dramas.

**Climax:** the turning point within the story; the moment of greatest tension that usually concludes the piece.

**Conflict:** the struggle between two forces within the story; this struggle may be internal or external.

**Dénouement:** the unraveling or part of the piece that contains resolution, final explanation, or clarification.

**Exposition:** the part of the piece that introduces the characters, setting, time, etc. to the reader.

**Flashback:** a literary device in which an earlier scene or event is inserted into the otherwise normal chronological order of a narrative.

**Foreshadowing:** the hints or suggestions within a text that indicate a future event that is yet to come.

**Freytag's Pyramid:** a diagram that describes the 5 parts of a drama, as explained by Freytag: exposition, rising action, climax, falling action, and dénouement. (*See schematic drawing.*)

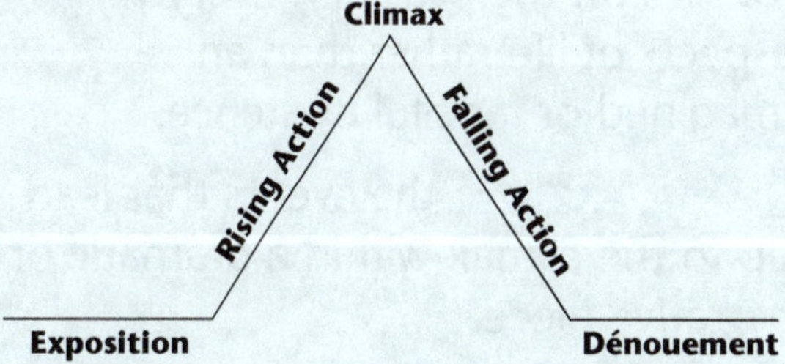


**Imagery:** the use of words to cause sensory images or impressions that go beyond the words used.

**Irony:** a literary device in which contradictory statements stand in contrast to what appears to be true or expected.

**Metaphor:** a comparison between two seemingly unlike things using *is* as the bridge. The verb may be omitted or implied.

**Memoir:** written as an autobiography, a memoir focuses attention on the author's interaction with historic events and his relationship with other significant historical players.

Copyright © Kendall Hunt Publishing Company

**Mood:** the emotional aspect of the piece that helps create a feeling within the audience.

**Poetic Justice:** a literary device in which virtue is rewarded and injustice punished. In more recent literature, authors often use an ironic twist of fate to create the outcome of punishment or reward.

**Point of View:** the perspective from which the story is told.

**Realism:** a form of literature that focuses on the ordinary, everyday aspects of life rather than an imagined or fanciful existence.

**Rising Action:** the events that lead up to the climax within a dramatic or narrative piece.

**Sarcasm:** this literary device falls into the classification of verbal irony at times.

**Setting:** the complete background or environment of a story. Geographic location, specific or local backdrops, and a sense of time and season are all elements of setting.

**Simile:** a comparison between two seemingly unlike things using *like* or *as* for the comparison bridge.

**Symbol:** an item, word, or image that represents something else by association, similarity, or convention.

**Theme:** the overriding or dominant idea in the story that is a universal statement about humanity. The most important message the author wishes the audience to take away or understand is the theme.

**Tone:** the atmosphere created by a writer regarding either his subject or his audience. A byproduct of the author's attitude, the tone of a literary work can range from defiant to accommodating.

**Transcendentalism:** American in nature, this philosophical movement flourished during the immediate quarter century before the Civil War. Primarily a movement that combined spiritual and philosophical aspects, Transcendentalism celebrated the individual and morality, rejected materialism, and focused on the gifts of nature. Transcendentalists chose to emphasize intuition as a path to knowledge and the reliance on feelings and self-perception as a way to find the divine.

Copyright © Kendall Hunt Publishing Company

# Glossary of Writing Terms

**Argument:** the written or spoken act of expressing one's point of view.

**Claim:** a statement that provides a belief or truth. In order to be strong, a claim must be supported by evidence.

**Ethos:** a way of using one's emotions as a speaker or writer in an attempt to persuade an audience.

**Evidence:** the information or material that is given to support an argument. In Toulmin's Model of Argumentation, the evidence provided to support a warrant is known as the *backing*. Further, in Toulmin's Model of Argumentation, the evidence that supports a claim or reason is known as the *grounds*.

**Logos:** a way of using arguments that appeal to the logic or reason of an audience.

**Pathos:** a way of using words to evoke the emotion the speaker or writer hopes to induce in the audience.

**Persuasion:** the act of trying to sway or change someone else's point of view.

**Reasons:** in argumentation, a reason expands the writer's claim by giving supportive evidence. In Toulmin's Model of Argumentation, the argument attaches the reason to the claim by a warrant.

**Thesis:** a succinctly stated sentence that states the writer's main point.

**Warrant:** the connection between a claim and the reasons, with data that support it.

Copyright © Kendall Hunt Publishing Company

# Models

The following pages include information about some models that you can use to help organize your thinking.

## The Taba Model of Concept Development

The concept development model, based upon Hilda Taba's Concept Development model (Taba, 1962), involves both inductive and deductive reasoning processes. Used as an early lesson in each unit, the model focuses on the creation of generalizations from a student-derived list of created concepts.

The model is comprised of five steps and involves student participation at every step. Students begin with a broad concept, determine specific examples from that, create appropriate categorization systems, establish a generalization from those categories and then apply the generalization to their readings and other situations.

This model is best employed by dividing the class into small groups of 4 to 5 for initial work, followed by whole class discussion after each stage of the process. The explanation below illustrates the use of the model around the concept of change, the central idea of some of the units.

1. Students generate examples of the concept of change, derived from their own understanding and experiences with changes in the world. Teachers should encourage students to provide at least 25 examples.
2. Once an adequate number of examples has been elicited, students then group examples together into categories. Such a process allows students to search for interrelatedness and to organize materials. Students should explain their reasoning for given categories and seek clarification from each other as a whole class. Teachers should ensure that students have accounted for all of their examples through the categories established.
3. Students are now asked to think of non-examples of the concept of change. Teachers may begin the brainstorming process with the direction, "Now list examples of things that do not change." Teachers should encourage students to think carefully about non-examples and discuss ideas within their groups. Each group should list five to six examples.

Copyright © Kendall Hunt Publishing Company

4. The students now determine generalizations about the concept of change, using their lists of examples and nonexamples. Generalizations might include such ideas as "Change may be positive or negative" and "Change is linked to time." Generalizations should be derived from student input and may not precisely reflect the unit generalizations. Teachers should post the students' best generalizations on one side of the room and the prescribed unit generalizations on the other. Each set should be referred to throughout the unit.
5. Throughout the unit, students are asked to identify specific examples of the generalizations from their own readings, or to describe how the concept of change applies to a given situation about which they have read. Students are also asked to apply the generalizations to their own writings and their own lives.

Source: Taba, H. (1962). *Curriculum development: Theory and practice.* NY: Harcourt, Brace & World, Inc.

Younger children may require a modified approach to the methodology listed above. The teacher may want to brainstorm with the whole group rather than dividing students into small groups. Additionally, student responses can be written on sentence strips or sticky notes that can be used during categorization. The sentence strips or sticky notes could then be physically sorted into the corresponding categories. This "physical sort," or tactile/kinesthetic approach, would facilitate the students' ability to move the responses among the different categories and their understanding of the concept and generalizations.

The concept development model provides a unifying means for students to gain an in-depth understanding within and across the literature pieces for each unit. Practice webs using the generalizations are structured into core lessons in the unit.

Source: Center for Gifted Education. (2013). *What Works: 25 years of commitment to gifted children through research and curriculum at the Center for Gifted Education at The College of William & Mary.* TX: Prufrock Press, Inc.

To enhance the learning experience of students, the selected concept and accompanying generalizations should extend into the students' other curricula. The more connections they are able to draw, the deeper they will be able to examine and understand the concept and generalizations.

Copyright © Kendall Hunt Publishing Company

The following is a list of concepts and related generalizations that have been used in units developed by the Center for Gifted Education:

### Courage

- Courage may be displayed by an individual, a group, or a society.
- Courage is not always apparent or even intended. Reflection often reveals the courageous side of actions.
- Courage may require a person to go against conventional or traditional patterns of behavior or thought.
- Courage or acts of courage may bring benefits to large groups of people. It may bring personal cost(s) to the person(s) displaying it.
- Courageous acts may be viewed as positive or negative.
- Courage may be mental, physical, social, spiritual, and/or emotional in nature.

### Change

- Change is everywhere.
- Change is linked to time.
- Change may be positive or negative.
- Change may be perceived as orderly or random.
- Change may happen naturally or be caused by people.

### Systems

- The interactions and outputs of a system change when its inputs, elements, or boundaries change.
- Systems can be productive or dysfunctional.
- Many systems are made up of smaller systems.
- Systems are interdependent.
- All systems have patterns.

Copyright © Kendall Hunt Publishing Company

## Perspective

- Perspective depends upon who it is that is encountering whatever object, event, or situation the perspective is about.
- Understanding of issues requires examination of different perspectives.
- Different people bring different perspectives to any situation based on their own experiences and assumptions about the world.
- The perspective from which something is presented influences our interpretation.
- The perspective held by individuals or groups can change over time.

## Authority

- Authority can be derived from a person or a position.
- The legitimacy of authority is grounded in the culture and values of that place and time.
- Enduring authority rests with institutions, not individuals.
- Authority is demonstrated through symbols, symbolic actions, and procedures.
- Authority changes in response to other expressions of power.

Copyright © Kendall Hunt Publishing Company

## Cause and Effect

- Causes may have predictable and unpredictable effects.
- Causes can trigger simple effects or chains of related effects.
- An effect can be the result of multiple causes with different degrees of influence.
- A relationship between events that seems to be cause-effect may actually be correlational or coincidental.
- Causes have short-term and long-term effects.
- Some effects have causes that are hidden when the event occurs but are discovered later through scientific or historical investigation.

## The Literature Web Model

The Literature Web is a model designed to guide interpretation of a literature selection by encouraging you to connect your personal response with elements of the text. The web may be completed independently and/or as a tool for discussion. The web has five parts:

1. **Key Words:** interesting, unfamiliar, striking, or particularly important words and phrases contained within the text
2. **Feelings:** the reader's feelings, with discussion of specific text details inspiring them; the characters' feelings; and the feelings the reader infers the author intended to inspire
3. **Ideas:** major themes and main ideas of the text; key concepts
4. **Images and Symbols:** notable sensory images in the text, "pictures" in the reader's mind and the text that inspired them, symbols for abstract ideas
5. **Structure:** the form and structure of the writing and how they contribute to meaning; may identify such features as use of unusual time sequence in narrative, such as flashbacks, use of voice, use of figurative language, etc.; style of writing

Copyright © Kendall Hunt Publishing Company

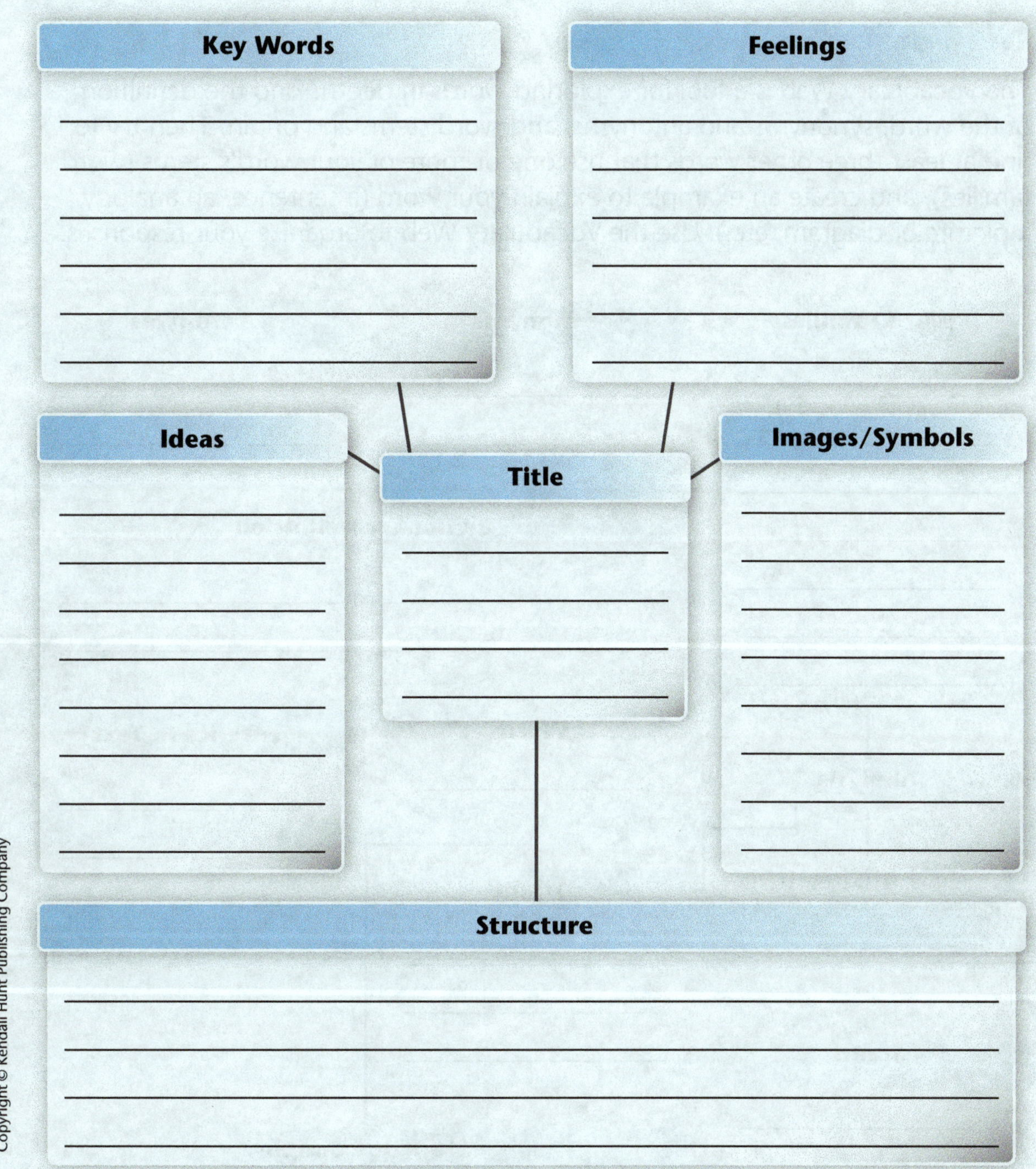


**Figure 1-1:** Literature Web Model

Copyright © Kendall Hunt Publishing Company

## The Vocabulary Web Model

The Vocabulary Web is a tool for exploring words in depth. Find the definition of the word, synonyms and antonyms, and word stems and origin. Then try to find at least three other words that use one or more of your word's stems (word families), and create an example to explain your word (a sentence, an analogy, a picture or diagram, etc.). Use the Vocabulary Web to organize your responses.

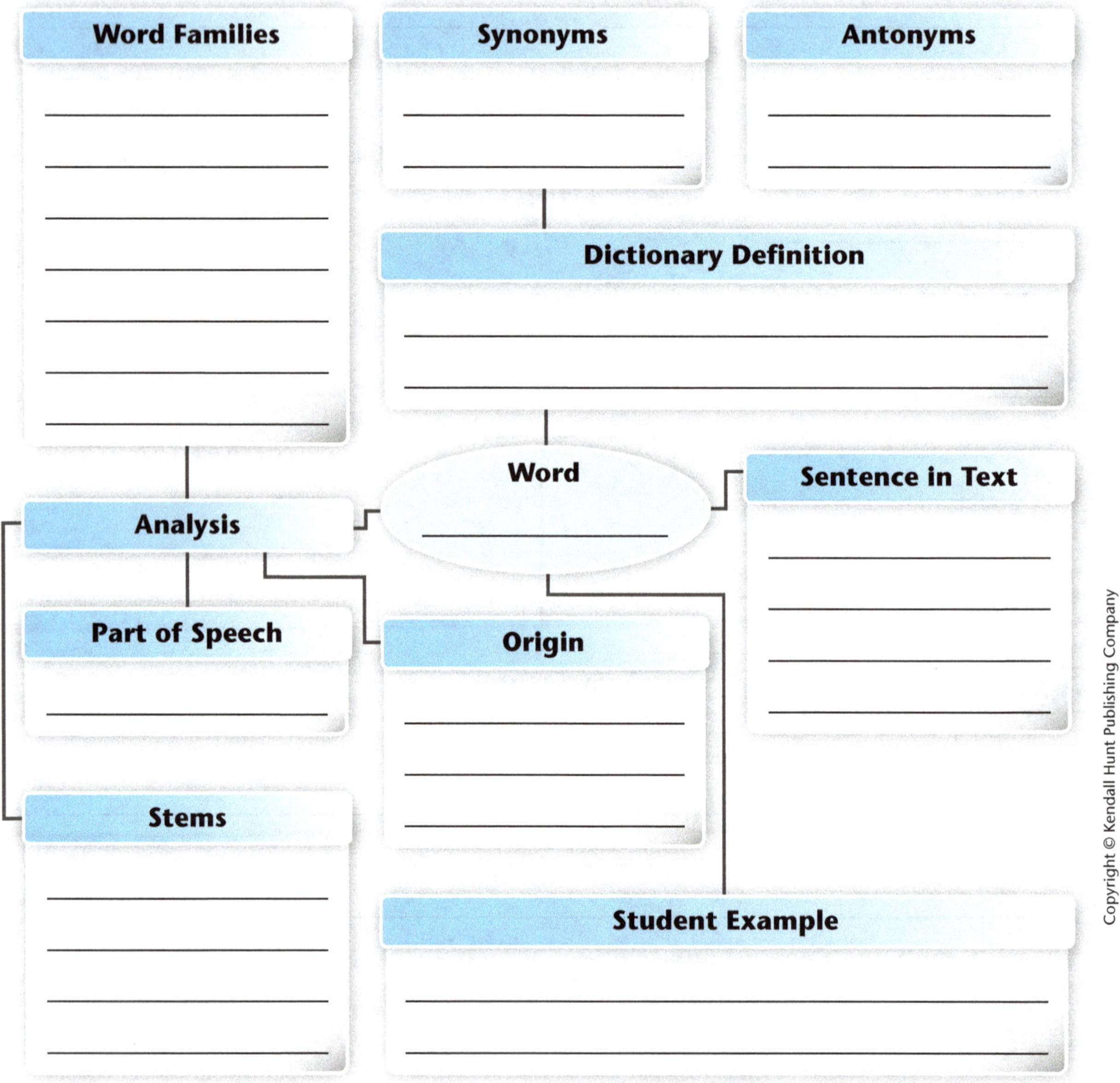


Figure 1-2: Vocabulary Web Model

Copyright © Kendall Hunt Publishing Company

# Unit Vocabulary List

## From "Defining Liberty":

liberty

## From "Disappointment Is the Lot of Women":

ephemeral

## From "The Valiant Chattee Maker":

banyan tree
bellicose
blunder
confiscate
decrepit
docile
eke
formidable
humble
intrepid
perpetual
Rajah/Maharajah
reconnaissance
resplendent
rogue
vex

## From *Of Mice and Men*:

aloof
apprehension
belligerent
bindle
cesspool
contemplate
crestfallen
derision
derogatory
drone
fawning
indignation
liniment
maul
mollify
monotonous
morose
mottled
ominous
pantomime
pugnacious
receptive
recumbent

Copyright © Kendall Hunt Publishing Company

reprehensible

reverence

reverently

rheumatism

woe

writhe

### From *No Promises in the Wind*:

ballyhoo

begrudged

brusque

callous

capricious

complacent

convalescence

decrepit

desolation

docile

imperceptible

improvident

improvisation

incredulously

indifferent

ingenuity

listless

loll

nonchalant

paltry

patronizing

pompous

ramshackle

rancor

ravine

resonant

sallow

sober

toil

tottered

### From *To Kill a Mockingbird*:

acquiescence

arid

assuage

auspicious

beadle

blandly

bovine

changelings

church

collards

connived

contentious

covey

crepey

deportment

dictum

doused

Copyright © Kendall Hunt Publishing Company

entailment
expunge
façade
fey
furtive
gait
heathen
hookahs
illicitly
impudent
ingenuous
invective
iota
irascible
jarred
lavations
mollified
myopic
obstreperous
passé
predilection
prowess
quelling
recluse
remorse
riled
rout
scrip stamps
shinny
smilax
snuff
statute
sundry
taut
temerity
tenet
tight
touchous
trousseau
venerable
wallowing
wary

## From *Warriors Don't Cry*:

accolades
adamant
anteroom
barrage
belligerent
chide
copious
deity
dither
edict
effigy
emaciated
enclave
fiasco

Copyright © Kendall Hunt Publishing Company

fracas
frivolity
gauntlet
impasse
impeccably
insolent
kowtow
livid
melee
moot
nonchalant
ominous
ostracized
placating
pristine
proviso
quash
respite
reverberate
tarry
tenacious
tolerable
trounced
unmitigated
veneer
vicarious

## From *The Night Thoreau Spent in Jail*:

abet
alacrity
conformity
dilemma
esteem
ethics
euphemism
expedient
fain
leaven
magnanimity
manipulate
motive
novel
perverted
posse comitatus
strait
sublime
superfluous
transcendentalism

Copyright © Kendall Hunt Publishing Company

# "Top Man"

## James Ramsey Ullman

Copyright © Kendall Hunt Publishing Company

**The gorge bent.** The walls fell suddenly away and we came out on the edge of a bleak, boulder-strewn valley. And there it was.

Osborn saw it first. He had been leading the column, threading his way slowly among the huge rock masses of the gorge's mouth. Then he came to the first flat, bare place and stopped. He neither pointed nor cried out, but every man behind him knew instantly what it was. The long file sprang taut, like a jerked rope. As swiftly as we could, but in complete silence, we came out into the open ground where Osborn stood, and raised our eyes with his. In the records of the Indian Topographical Survey it says:

Kalpurtha: a mountain in the Himalayas, altitude 28,900 ft. The highest peak in British India and fourth highest in the world. Also known as K3. A Tertiary formation of sedimentary limestone—

There were men among us who had spent months of their lives—in some cases, years—reading, thinking, planning about what now lay before us, but at that moment statistics and geology, knowledge, thought and plans, were as remote and forgotten as the faraway western cities from which we had come. We were men bereft of everything but eyes, everything but the single, electric perception: There it was!

Before us the valley stretched away into miles of rocky desolation. To right and left it was bounded by low ridges which, as the eye followed them, slowly mounted and drew closer together until the valley was no longer a valley at all, but a narrowing, rising corridor between the cliffs. What happened then I can describe only as a single, stupendous crash of music. At the end of the corridor and above it—so far above it that it shut out half the sky—hung the blinding white mass of K3.

It was like the many pictures I had seen, and at the same time utterly unlike them. The

© 1939, 1941, 1944, 1945, 1948, 1951, 1952, 1953 by James Ramsey Ullman. © renewed in 1967, 1969, 1972, 1973, 1976, 1979, 1980, 1981 by James Ramsey Ullman and the Estate of James Ramsey Ullman.

shape was there, and the familiar distinguishing features—the sweeping skirt of glaciers; the monstrous vertical precipices of the face and the jagged ice line of the east ridge; finally the symmetrical summit pyramid that transfixed the sky. But whereas in the pictures the mountain had always seemed unreal—a dream image of cloud, snow and crystal—it was now no longer an image at all. It was a mass, solid, imminent, appalling. We were still too far away to see the windy whipping of its snow plumes or to hear the cannonading of its avalanches, but in that sudden silent moment every man of us was for the first time aware of it, not as a picture in his mind but as a thing, an antagonist. For all its twenty eight thousand feet of lofty grandeur, it seemed, somehow, less to tower than to crouch—a white-hooded giant, secret and remote, but living. Living and on guard.

I turned my eyes from the dazzling glare and looked at my companions. Osborn still stood a little in front of the others. He was absolutely motionless, his young face tense and shining, his eyes devouring the mountain as a lover's might devour the face of his beloved. One could feel in the very set of his body the overwhelming desire that swelled in him to act, to come to grips, to conquer. A little behind him were ranged the other white men of the expedition: Randolph, our leader, Wittmer and Johns, Doctor Schlapp and Bixler. All were still, their eyes cast upward. Off to one side a little stood Nace, the Englishman, the only one among us who was not staring at K3 for the first time. He had been the last to come up out of the gorge and stood now with arms folded on his chest, squinting at the great peak he had known so long and fought so tirelessly and fiercely. His lean British face, under its mask of stubble and windburn, was expressionless. His lips were a colorless line, and his eyes seemed almost shut. Behind the sahibs ranged the porters, bent over their staffs, their brown, seamed faces straining upward from beneath their loads.

For a long while no one spoke or moved. The only sounds between earth and sky were the soft hiss of our breathing and the pounding of our hearts.

Through the long afternoon we wound slowly between the great boulders of the valley and at sundown pitched camp in the bed of a dried-up stream. The porters ate their rations in silence, wrapped themselves in their blankets and fell asleep under the

Copyright © Kendall Hunt Publishing Company

stars. The rest of us, as was our custom, sat close about the fire that blazed in the circle of tents, discussing the events of the day and the plans for the next. It was a flawlessly clear Himalayan night and K3 tiered up into the blackness like a monstrous sentinel lighted from within. There was no wind, but a great tide of cold air crept down the valley from the ice fields above, penetrating our clothing, pressing gently against the canvas of the tents.

"Another night or two and we'll be needing the sleeping bags," commented Randolph.

Osborn nodded. "We could use them tonight, would be my guess."

Randolph turned to Nace. "What do you say, Martin?"

The Englishman puffed at his pipe a moment. "Rather think it might be better to wait," he said at last.

"Wait? Why?" Osborn jerked his head up.

"Well, it gets pretty nippy high up, you know. I've seen it thirty below at twenty-five thousand on the east ridge. Longer we wait for the bags, better acclimated we'll get."

Osborn snorted. "A lot of good being acclimated will do if we have frozen feet."

"Easy, Paul, easy," cautioned Randolph. "It seems to me Martin's right."

Osborn bit his lip, but said nothing. The other men entered the conversation, and soon it had veered to other matters: the weather, the porters and pack animals, routes, camps and strategy—the inevitable, inexhaustible topics of the climber's world.

There were all kinds of men among the eight of us, men with a great diversity of background and interest. Sayre Randolph, whom the Alpine Club had named leader of our expedition, had for years been a well-known explorer and lecturer. Now in his middle fifties, he was no longer equal to the grueling physical demands of high climbing, but served as planner and organizer of the enterprise. Wittmer was a Seattle lawyer, who had recently made a name for himself by a series of difficult ascents in the Coast Range of British Columbia. Johns was an Alaskan, a fantastically strong, able sourdough, who had been a ranger in the U.S. Forest Service and had accompanied many famous Alaskan expeditions. Schlapp was a practicing physician from Milwaukee, Bixler a government meteorologist with

Copyright © Kendall Hunt Publishing Company

a talent for photography. I, at the time, was an assistant professor of geology at an eastern university.

Finally, and preëminently, there were Osborn and Nace. I say "preëminently," because even at this time, when we had been together as a party for little more than a month, I believe all of us realized that these were the two key men of our venture. None, to my knowledge, ever expressed it in words, but the conviction was there, nevertheless, that if any of us were eventually to stand on the hitherto unconquered summit of K3, it would be one of them, or both. They were utterly dissimilar men. Osborn was twenty-three and a year out of college, a compact, buoyant mass of energy and high spirits. He seemed to be wholly unaffected by either the physical or mental hazards of mountaineering and had already, by virtue of many spectacular ascents in the Alps and Rockies, won a reputation as the most skilled and audacious of younger American climbers. Nace was in his forties—lean, taciturn, introspective. An official in the Indian Civil Service, he had explored and climbed in the Himalayas for twenty years. He had been a member of all five of the unsuccessful British expeditions to K3, and in his last attempt had attained to within five hundred feet of the summit, the highest point which any man had reached on the unconquered giant. This had been the famous tragic attempt in which his fellow climber and life-long friend, Captain Furness, had slipped and fallen ten thousand feet to his death. Nace rarely mentioned his name, but on the steel head of his ice ax were engraved the words: TO MARTIN FROM JOHN. If fate were to grant that the ax of any one of us should be planted upon the summit of K3, I hoped it would be his.

Such were the men who huddled about the fire in the deep, still cold of that Himalayan night. There were many differences among us, in temperament as well as in background. In one or two cases, notably that of Osborn and Nace, there had already been a certain amount of friction, and as the venture continued and the struggles and hardships of the actual ascent began, it would, I knew, increase. But differences were unimportant. What mattered—all that mattered—was that our purpose was one—to conquer the monster of rock and ice that now loomed above us in the night; to stand for a moment where no man, no living thing,

Copyright © Kendall Hunt Publishing Company

had ever stood before. To that end we had come from half a world away, across oceans and continents to the fastnesses of inner Asia. To that end we were prepared to endure cold, exhaustion and danger, even to the very last extremity of human endurance. Why? There is no answer, and at the same time every man among us knew the answer; every man who has ever looked upon a great mountain and felt the fever in his blood to climb and conquer, knows the answer. George Leigh Mallory, greatest of mountaineers, expressed it once and for all when he was asked why he wanted to climb unconquered Everest. "I want to climb it," said Mallory, "because it's there."

Day after day we crept on and upward. The naked desolation of the valley was unrelieved by any motion, color or sound, and, as we progressed, it was like being trapped at the bottom of a deep well or in a sealed court between great skyscrapers. Soon we were thinking of the ascent of the shining mountain not only as an end in itself but as an escape.

In our nightly discussions around the fire, our conversation narrowed more and more to the immediate problems confronting us, and during them I began to realize that the tension between Osborn and Nace went deeper than I had at first surmised. There was rarely any outright argument between them—they were both far too able mountain men to disagree on fundamentals—but I saw that at almost every turn they were rubbing each other the wrong way. It was a matter of personalities chiefly. Osborn was talkative, enthusiastic, optimistic, always chafing to be up and at it, always wanting to take the short, straight line to the given point. Nace, on the other hand, was matter-of-fact, cautious, slow. He was the apostle of trial-and-error and watchful waiting. Because of his far greater experience and intimate knowledge of K3, Randolph almost invariably followed his advice, rather than Osborn's, when a difference of opinion arose. The younger man usually capitulated with good grace, but I could tell that he was irked.

During the days in the valley I had few occasions to talk privately with either of them, and only once did either mention the other in any but the most casual manner. Even then, the remarks they made seemed unimportant, and I remember them only in view of what happened later.

My conversation with Osborn occurred first. It was while we were on the march, and Osborn,

Copyright © Kendall Hunt Publishing Company

who was directly behind me, came up suddenly to my side.

"You're a geologist, Frank," he began without preamble. "What do you think of Nace's theory about the ridge?"

"What theory?" I asked.

"He believes we should traverse under it from the glacier up. Says the ridge itself is too exposed."

"It looks pretty mean through the telescope."

"But it's been done before. He's done it himself. All right, it's tough—I'll admit that. But a decent climber could make it in half the time the traverse will take."

"Nace knows the traverse is longer," I said, "but he seems certain it will be much easier for us."

"Easier for him is what he means." Osborn paused, looking moodily at the ground. "He was a great climber in his day. It's a damn shame a man can't be honest enough with himself to know when he's through." He fell silent and a moment later dropped back into his place in line.

It was that same night, I think, that I awoke to find Nace sitting up in his blanket and staring at the mountain.

"How clear it is," I whispered.

The Englishman pointed. "See the ridge?"

I nodded, my eyes fixed on the great, twisting spine of ice that climbed into the sky. I could see now, more clearly than in the blinding sunlight, its huge indentations and jagged, wind-swept pitches.

"It looks impossible," I said.

"No, it can be done. Trouble is, when you've made it, you're too done in for the summit."

"Osborn seems to think its shortness would make up for its difficulty."

Nace was silent a long moment before answering. Then for the first and only time I heard him speak the name of his dead companion. "That's what Furness thought," he said quietly. Then he lay down and wrapped himself in his blanket.

For the next two weeks the uppermost point of the valley was our home and workshop. We established our base camp as close to the mountain as we could, less than half a mile from the tongue of its lowest glacier, and plunged into the arduous tasks of preparation for the ascent. Our food and equipment were unpacked, inspected and sorted, and finally repacked in lighter loads for transportation to more

Copyright © Kendall Hunt Publishing Company

advanced camps. Hours on end were spent poring over maps and charts and studying the monstrous heights above us through telescope and binoculars. Under Nace's supervision, a thorough reconnaissance of the glacier was made and the route across it laid out; then began the backbreaking labor of moving up supplies and establishing the advance stations.

Camps I and II were set up on the glacier itself, in the most sheltered sites we could find. Camp III we built at its upper end, as near as possible to the point where the great rock spine of K3 thrust itself free of ice and began its precipitous ascent. According to our plans, this would be the advance base of operations during the climb; the camps to be established higher up, on the mountain proper, would be too small and too exposed to serve as anything more than one or two nights' shelter. The total distance between the base camp and Camp III was only fifteen miles, but the utmost daily progress of our porters was five miles, and it was essential that we should never be more than twelve hours' march from food and shelter. Hour after hour, day after day, the long file of men wound up and down among the hummocks and crevasses of the glacier, and finally the time arrived when we were ready to advance.

Leaving Doctor Schlapp in command of eight porters at the base camp, we proceeded easily and on schedule, reaching Camp I the first night, Camp II the second and the advance base the third. No men were left at Camps I and II, inasmuch as they were designed simply as caches for food and equipment; and, furthermore, we knew we would need all the man power available for the establishment of the higher camps on the mountain proper.

For more than three weeks now the weather had held perfectly, but on our first night at the advance base, as if by malignant prearrangement of Nature, we had our first taste of the supernatural fury of a high Himalayan storm. It began with great streamers of lightning that flashed about the mountain like a halo; then heavily through the weird glare snow began to fall. The wind howled about the tents with hurricane frenzy, and the wild flapping of the canvas dinned in our ears like machine-gun fire.

There was no sleep for us that night or the next. For thirty-six hours the storm raged without lull, while we huddled in the icy

Copyright © Kendall Hunt Publishing Company

gloom of the tents. At last, on the third morning, it was over, and we came out into a world transformed by a twelve foot cloak of snow. No single landmark remained as it had been before, and our supplies and equipment were in the wildest confusion. Fortunately, there had not been a single serious injury, but it was another three days before we had regained our strength and put the camp in order.

Then we waited. The storm did not return, and the sky beyond the ridges gleamed flawlessly clear, but night and day we could hear the roaring thunder of avalanches on the mountain above us. To have ventured so much as one step into that savage, vertical wilderness before the new-fallen snow froze tight would have been suicidal. We chafed or waited patiently, according to our individual temperaments, while the days dragged by.

It was late one afternoon that Osborn returned from a short reconnaissance up the ridge. His eyes were shining and his voice jubilant.

"It's tight!" he cried. "Tight as a drum! We can go!" All of us stopped whatever we were doing. His excitement leaped like an electric spark from one to another. "I went about a thousand feet, and it's sound all the way. What do you say, Sayre? Tomorrow?"

Randolph hesitated a moment, then looked at Nace.

"Better give it another day or two," said the Englishman.

Osborn glared at him. "Why?" he challenged.

"It's generally safer to wait until—"

"Wait! Wait!" Osborn exploded. "Don't you ever think of anything but waiting? The snow's firm, I tell you!"

"It's firm down here," Nace replied quietly, "because the sun hits it only two hours a day. Up above it gets the sun twelve hours. It may not have frozen yet."

"The avalanches have stopped."

"That doesn't necessarily mean it will hold a man's weight."

"It seems to me, Martin's point —" Randolph began.

Osborn wheeled on him. "Sure," he snapped. "I know. Martin's right. The cautious bloody English are always right. Let him have his way, and we'll be sitting here twiddling our thumbs until the mountain falls down on us." His eyes flashed to Nace. "Maybe with a little less of that bloody cautiousness, you English wouldn't have made such a mess of Everest. Maybe your pals Mallory and Furness wouldn't be dead."

Copyright © Kendall Hunt Publishing Company

"Osborn!" commanded Randolph sharply.

The youngster stared at Nace for another moment, breathing heavily. Then, abruptly, he turned away.

The next two days were clear and windless, but we still waited, following Nace's advice. There were no further brushes between him and Osborn, but an unpleasant air of restlessness and tension hung over the camp. I found myself chafing almost as impatiently as Osborn himself for the moment when we would break out of that maddening inactivity and begin the assault.

At last the day came. With the first paling of the sky, a roped file of men, bent almost double beneath heavy loads, began slowly to climb the ice slope just beneath the jagger line of the great east ridge. In accordance with prearranged plan, we proceeded in relays; this first group consisting of Nace, Johns, myself and eight porters. It was our job to ascend approximately two thousand feet in a day's climbing and establish Camp IV at the most level and sheltered site we could find. We would spend the night there and return to the advance base next day, while the second relay, consisting of Osborn, Wittemer and eight more porters, went up with their loads. This process was to continue until all necessary supplies were at Camp IV, and then the whole thing would be repeated between Camps IV and V, and V and VI. From VI, at an altitude of about 26,000 feet, the ablest and fittest men—presumable Nace and Osborn—would make the direct assault on the summit. Randolph and Bixler were to remain at the advance base throughout the operations, acting as directors and coördinators. We were under the strictest orders that any man, sahib or porter, who suffered illness or injury should be brought down immediately.

How shall I describe those next two weeks beneath the great ice ridge of K3? In a sense, there was no occurrence of importance, and at the same time everything happened that could possibly happen, short of actual disaster. We established Camp IV, came down again, went up again, came down again. Then we crept laboriously higher. The wind increased, and the air grew steadily colder and more difficult to breathe. One morning two of the porters awoke with their feet frozen black; they had to be sent down. A short while later Johns developed an uncontrollable nosebleed and was forced to descend to a lower

Copyright © Kendall Hunt Publishing Company

camp. Wittmer was suffering from splitting headaches and I from continually dry throat. But providentially, the one enemy we feared the most in that icy, gale-lashed hell did not again attack us—no snow fell. And day by day, foot by foot, we ascended.

It is during ordeals like this that the surface trappings of a man are shed and his secret mettle laid bare. There were no shirkers or quitters among us—I had known that from the beginning—but now, with each passing day, it became more manifest which were the strongest and ablest among us. Beyond all argument, these were Osborn and Nace.

Osborn was magnificent. All the boyish impatience and moodiness which he had exhibited earlier were gone, and now that he was at last at work in his natural element, he emerged as the peerless mountaineer he was. His energy was inexhaustible, and his speed, both on rock and ice, almost twice that of any other man in the party. He was always discovering new routes and short cuts; and there was such vigor, buoyancy and youth in everything he did that it gave heart to the rest of us.

In contrast, Nace was slow, methodical, unspectacular. Since he and I worked in the same relay, I was with him almost constantly, and to this day I carry in my mind the clear image of the man—his tall body bent almost double against endless, shimmering slops of ice; his lean brown face bent in utter concentration on the problem in hand, then raised searchingly to the next; the bright prong of his ax rising, falling with tireless rhythm, until the steps in the glassy incline were so wide and deep that the most clumsy of the porters could not have slipped from them had he tried. Osborn attacked the mountain, head on. Nace studied it, sparred with it, wore it down. His spirit did not flap from his sleeve like a pennon; it was deep inside him, patient, indomitable.

The day came soon when I learned from him what it is to be a great mountaineer. We were making the ascent from Camp IV to V, and an almost perpendicular ice wall had made it necessary for us to come out for a few yards on the exposed crest of the ridge. There were six of us in the party, roped together, with Nace leading, myself second, and four porters bringing up the rear. The ridge at this particular point was free of snow, but razor-thin, and the rocks were covered with a smooth glaze of ice. On either side the mountain dropped away in sheer precipices of five thousand feet.

Copyright © Kendall Hunt Publishing Company

Suddenly the last porter slipped. In what seemed to be the same instant I heard the ominous scraping of boot nails and, turning, saw a wildly gesticulating figure plunge sideways into the abyss. There was a scream as the next porter followed him. I remember trying frantically to dig into the ridge with my ax, realizing at the same time it would no more hold against the weight of the falling men than a pin stuck in a wall. Then I heard Nace shout, "Jump!" As he said it, the rope went tight about my waist, and I went hurtling after him into space on the opposite side of the ridge. After me came the nearest porter.

What happened then must have happened in five yards and a fifth of a second. I heard myself cry out, and the glacier, a mile below, rushed up at me, spinning. Then both were blotted out in a violent spasm, as the rope jerked taut. I hung for a moment, an inert mass, feeling that my body had been cut in two; then I swung in slowly to the side of the mountain. Above me the rope lay tight and motionless across the crest of the ridge, our weight exactly counter-balancing that of the men who had fallen on the far slope.

Nace's voice came up from below. "You chaps on the other side!" he shouted. "Start climbing slowly! We're climbing too!"

In five minutes we had all regained the ridge. The porters and I crouched panting on the jagged rocks, our eyes closed, the sweat beading our faces in frozen drops. Nace carefully examined the rope that again hung loosely between us.

"All right, men," he said presently. "Let's get on to camp for a cup of tea."

Above Camp V the whole aspect of the ascent changed. The angle of the ridge eased off, and the ice, which lower down had covered the mountain like a sheath, lay only in scattered patches between the rocks. Fresh enemies, however, instantly appeared to take the place of the old. We were now laboring at an altitude of more than 25,000 feet—well above the summits of the highest surrounding peaks—and day and night, without protection or respite, we were buffeted by the savage fury of the wind. Worse than this was that the atmosphere had become so rarefied it could scarcely support life. Breathing itself was a major physical effort, and our progress upward consisted of two or three painful steps, followed by a long period of rest in which our hearts pounded wildly

Copyright © Kendall Hunt Publishing Company

and our burning lungs gasped for air. Each of us carried a small cylinder of oxygen in our pack, but we used it only in emergencies, and found that, though its immediate effect was salutary, it left us later even worse off than before.

But the great struggle was now mental rather than physical. The lack of air induced a lethargy of mind and spirit; confidence and the powers of thought and decision waned. The mountain, to all of us, was no longer a mere giant of rock and ice; it had become a living thing, an enemy, watching us, waiting for us, hostile, relentless.

On the fifteenth day after we had first left the advance base, we pitched Camp VI at an altitude of 26,500 feet. It was located near the uppermost extremity of the great east ridge, directly beneath the so-called shoulder of the mountain. On the far side of the shoulder the stupendous north face of K3 fell sheer to the glaciers, two miles below. Above it and to the left rose the symmetrical bulk of the summit pyramid. The topmost rocks of its highest pinnacle were clearly visible from the shoulder, and the intervening fifteen hundred feet seemed to offer no insuperable obstacles.

Camp VI, which was in reality no camp at all but a single tent, was large enough to accommodate only three men. Osborn established it with the aid of Wittmer and one porter; then, the following morning, Wittmer and the porter descended to Camp V, and Nace and I went up. It was our plan that Osborn and Nace should launch the final assault—the next day, if the weather held—with myself in support, following their progress through binoculars and going to their aid or summoning help from below if anything went wrong. As the three of us lay in the tent that night, the summit seemed already within arm's reach, victory securely in our grasp.

And then the blow fell. With fiendishly malignant timing, which no power on earth could have made us believe was a simple accident of nature, the mountain hurled at us its last line of defense. It snowed.

For a day and a night the great flakes drove down upon us, swirling and swooping in the wind, blotting out the summit, the shoulder, everything beyond the tiny white-walled radius of our tent. At last, during the morning of the following day, it cleared. The sun came out in a thin blue sky, and the summit pyramid again appeared above us, now whitely robed in fresh snow. But still we

Copyright © Kendall Hunt Publishing Company

waited. Until the snow either froze or was blown away by the wind, it would have been the rashest courting of destruction for us to have ascended a foot beyond the camp. Another day passed. And another.

By the third nightfall our nerves were at the breaking point. For hours on end we had scarcely moved or spoken, and the only sounds in all the world were the endless moaning of the wind outside and the harsh, sucking noise of our breathing. I knew that, one way or another, the end had come. Our meager food supply was running out; even with careful rationing, there was enough left for only two more days.

Presently Nace stirred in his sleeping bag and sat up. "We'll have to go down tomorrow," he said quietly.

For a moment there was silence in the tent. Then Osborn struggled to a sitting position and faced him.

"No," he said.

"There's still too much loose snow above. We can't make it."

"But it's clear. As long as we can see—"

Nace shook his head. "Too dangerous. We'll go down tomorrow and lay in a fresh supply. Then we'll try again."

"Once we go down we're licked. You know it."

Nace shrugged. "Better to be licked than—" The strain of speech was suddenly too much for him and he fell into a violent paroxysm of coughing. When it had passed, there was a long silence.

Then, suddenly, Osborn spoke again. "Look, Nace," he said, "I'm going up tomorrow."

The Englishman shook his head.

"I'm going—understand?"

For the first time since I had known him, I saw Nace's eyes flash in anger. "I'm the senior member of this group," he said. "I forbid you to go!"

With a tremendous effort, Osborn jerked himself to his feet. "You forbid me? This may be your sixth time on this mountain, and all that, but you don't own it! I know what you're up to. You haven't got it in you to make the top yourself, so you don't want anyone else to get the glory. That's it, isn't it? Isn't it?" He sat down again suddenly, gasping for breath.

Nace looked at him with level eyes. "This mountain has licked me five times," he said softly. "It killed my best friend. It means more to me to lick it than anything else in the world. Maybe I'll make it and maybe I won't. But if I do, it will be as a rational, intelligent human being, not as a damned fool throwing my life away—"

Copyright © Kendall Hunt Publishing Company

He collapsed into another fit of coughing and fell back in his sleeping bag. Osborn, too, was still. They lay there inert, panting, too exhausted for speech.

It was hours later that I awoke from dull, uneasy sleep. In the faint light I saw Nace fumbling with the flap of the tent.

"What is it?" I asked.

"Osborn. He's gone."

The words cut like a blade through my lethargy. I struggled to my feet and followed Nace from the tent.

Outside, the dawn was seeping up the eastern sky. It was very cold, but the wind had fallen and the mountain seemed to hang suspended in a vast stillness. Above us the summit pyramid climbed bleakly into space, like the last outpost of a spent lifeless planet. Raising my binoculars, I swept them over the gray waste. At first I saw nothing but rock and ice; then, suddenly, something moved.

"I've got him," I whispered.

As I spoke, the figure of Osborn sprang into clear focus against a patch of ice. He took three or four slow upward steps, stopped, went on again. I handed the glasses to Nace.

The Englishman squinted through them a moment, returned them to me and re-entered the tent. When I followed, he had already laced his boots and was pulling on his outer gloves.

"He's not far," he said. "Can't have been gone more than half an hour." He seized his ice ax and started out again.

"Wait," I said. "I'm going with you."

Nace shook his head. "Better stay here."

"I'm going with you," I said.

He said nothing further, but waited while I made ready. In a few moments we left the tent, roped up and started off.

Almost immediately we were on the shoulder and confronted with the paralyzing two-mile drop of the north face, but we negotiated the short exposed stretch without mishap and in ten minutes were working up the base of the summit pyramid. Our progress was creepingly slow. There seemed to be literally no air at all to breathe, and after almost every step we were forced to rest.

The minutes crawled into hours, and still we climbed. Presently the sun came up. Its level rays streamed across the clouds far below, and glinted from the summits of distant peaks. But, although the pinnacle of K3 soared a full five thousand feet above anything in the surrounding world, we had scarcely any sense of

Copyright © Kendall Hunt Publishing Company

height. The stupendous wilderness of mountains and glaciers that spread beneath us to the horizon was flattened and remote, an unreal, insubstantial landscape seen in a dream. We had no connection with it, or it with us. All living, all awareness, purpose and will, was concentrated in the last step and the next—to put one foot before the other; to breathe; to ascend. We struggled on in silence.

I do not know how long it was since we had left the camp—it might have been two hours, it might have been six—when we suddenly sighted Osborn. We had not been able to find him again since our first glimpse through the binoculars, but now, unexpectedly and abruptly, as we came up over a jagged outcropping of rock, there he was. He was at a point, only a few yards above us, where the mountain steepened into an almost vertical wall. The smooth surface directly in front of him was obviously unclimbable, but two alternate routes were presented. To the left, a chimney cut obliquely across the wall, forbiddingly steep, but seeming to offer adequate holds. To the right was a gentle slope of snow that curved upward and out of sight behind the rocks. As we watched, Osborn ascended to the edge of the snow, stopped and tested it with his foot; then, apparently satisfied that it would bear his weight, he stepped out on the slope.

I felt Nace's body tense. "Paul!" he cried out.

His voice was too weak and hoarse to carry. Osborn continued his ascent.

Nace cupped his hands and called his name again, and this time Osborn turned. "Wait!" cried the Englishman.

Osborn stood still, watching us, as we struggled up the few yards to the edge of the snow slope. Nace's breath came in shuddering gasps, but he climbed faster than I had ever seen him climb before.

"Come back!" he called. "Come off the snow!"

"It's all right! The crust is firm!" Osborn called back.

"But it's melting! There's"—Nace paused, fighting for air—"there's nothing underneath!"

In a sudden, horrifying flash I saw what he meant. Looked at from directly below, at the point where Osborn had come to it, the slope on which he stood appeared as a harmless covering of snow over the rocks. From where we were now, however, a little to one side, it could be seen that it was in reality no covering at all, but merely a cornice or unsupported platform clinging to the side of the

Copyright © Kendall Hunt Publishing Company

mountain. Below it was not rock, but ten thousand feet of blue air.

"Come back!" I cried. "Come back!"

Osborn hesitated, then took a downward step. But he never took the next. For in that same instant the snow directly in front of him disappeared. It did not seem to fall or to break away. It was just soundlessly and magically no longer there. In the spot where Osborn had been about to set his foot there was now revealed the abysmal drop of the north face of K3.

I shut my eyes, but only for a second, and when I reopened them Osborn was still, miraculously, there.

Nace was shouting, "Don't move! Don't move an inch!"

"The rope," I heard myself saying.

The Englishman shook his head. "We'd have to throw it, and the impact would be too much. Brace yourself and play it out." As he spoke, his eyes were traveling over the rocks that bordered the snow bridge. Then he moved forward.

I wedged myself into a cleft in the wall and let out the rope which extended between us. A few yards away, Osborn stood in the snow, transfixed, one foot a little in front of the other. But my eyes now were on Nace. Cautiously, but with astonishing rapidity, he edged along the rocks beside the cornice. There was a moment when his only support was an inch-wide ledge beneath his feet, another where there was nothing under his feet at all and he supported himself wholly by his elbows and hands. But he advanced steadily, and at last reached a shelf wide enough for him to turn around on. At this point he was perhaps six feet away from Osborn.

"It's wide enough here to hold both of us," he said in a quiet voice. "I'm going to reach out my ax. Don't move until you're sure you have a grip on it. When I pull, jump."

He searched the wall behind him and found a hold for his left hand. Then he slowly extended his ice ax, head foremost, until it was within two feet of Osborn's shoulder.

"Grip it!" he cried suddenly Osborn's hands shot out and seized the ax. "Jump!"

There was a flash of steel in the sunlight and a hunched figure hurtled inward from the snow to the ledge. Simultaneously another figure hurtled out. The haft of the ax jerked suddenly from Nace's hand, and he lurched forward and downward. A violent, sickening spasm convulsed my body as the rope went taut. Then it was

Copyright © Kendall Hunt Publishing Company

gone. Nace did not seem to hit the snow; he simply disappeared through it, soundlessly. In the same instant the snow itself was gone. The frayed, yellow end of broken rope spun lazily in space.

Somehow my eyes went to Osborn. He was crouched on the ledge where Nace had been a moment before, staring dully at the ax he held in his hands. Beyond his head, not two hundred feet above, the white, untrodden pinnacle of K3 stabbed the sky.

Perhaps ten minutes passed, perhaps a half hour. I closed my eyes and leaned forward motionless against the rock, my face against my arm. I neither thought nor felt; my body and mind alike were enveloped in a suffocating numbness. Through it at last came the sound of Osborn moving. Looking up, I saw he was standing beside me.

"I'm going to try to make the top," he said tonelessly.

I merely stared at him.

"Will you come?"

I shook my head slowly. Osborn hesitated a moment, then turned and began slowly climbing the steep chimney above us. Halfway up he paused, struggling for breath. Then he resumed his laborious upward progress and presently disappeared beyond the crest.

I stayed where I was, and the hours passed. The sun reached its zenith above the peak and sloped away behind it. And at last I heard above me the sound of Osborn returning. As I looked up, his figure appeared at the top of the chimney and began the descent. His clothing was in tatters, and I could tell from his movements that only the thin flame of his will stood between him and collapse. In another few minutes he was standing beside me.

"Did you get there?" I asked.

He shook his head slowly. "I couldn't make it," he answered. "I didn't have what it takes."

We roped together silently and began the descent to the camp. There is nothing more to be told of the sixth assault on K3—at least not from the experiences of the men who made it. Osborn and I reached Camp V in safety, and three days later the entire expedition gathered at the advance base. It was decided, in view of the appalling tragedy that had occurred , to make no further attempt on the summit, and we began the evacuation of the mountain.

It remained for another year and other men to reveal the epilogue.

The summer following our attempt a combined English-Swiss

Copyright © Kendall Hunt Publishing Company

expedition stormed the peak successfully. After weeks of hardship and struggle, they attained the topmost pinnacle of the giant, only to find that what should have been their great moment of triumph was, instead, a moment of the bitterest disappointment. For when they came out at last upon the summit, they saw that they were not the first. An ax stood there. Its haft was embedded in rock and ice, and on its steel head were the engraved words: TO MARTIN FROM JOHN.

They were sporting men. On their return to civilization they told their story, and the name of the conqueror of K3 was made known to the world.

Copyright © Kendall Hunt Publishing Company

Name: ______________________________ Date: ______________

# Sample Response Journal Prompts

The following are some prompts you can use to help make connections between yourself and the text.

- *The justice in the story was similar to the time…*
- *That made me think of the time…*
- *I can relate…*
- *Make a connection between this text and other texts.*
- *This part is just like…*
- *That reminds me of…*
- *I read another book where…*
- *This is similar to…*
- *Make a connection between the text and other things you know.*
- *That reminds me of…*
- *This is like…*
- *I know about this … but I didn't know that.*
- *Write about the character(s), events, or setting.*
- *Write about the important ideas.*
- *Write about something new you learned.*
- *Does a character or scene in this book have any qualities as in real life?*
- *What character did you feel most happy for? Why?*
- *What character did you identify with or feel the most sympathy for? What is it about the character that made you feel this way?*
- *State your feelings, thoughts, reactions, and questions about situations, ideas, actions, character, setting, symbols, plot, theme, and any other elements of the book.*

Copyright © Kendall Hunt Publishing Company

## 2A Sample Response Journal Prompts (Continued)

- *Write about what you like or dislike, what seems confusing, or what seems unusual to you.*
- *Tell what you think something means.*
- *Make predictions about what might happen later.*
- *Relate your personal experiences that connect with the plot, characters or setting.*
- *How do these characters show progress? What points showed a regression?*

Copyright © Kendall Hunt Publishing Company

Name: ______________________ Date: ______________

# Literature Web

**Directions:** Complete a Literature Web for "Top Man."

| Key Words | Feelings |
|---|---|
| | |

| Ideas | Title | Images/Symbols |
|---|---|---|
| | | |

| Structure |
|---|
| |

Copyright © Kendall Hunt Publishing Company

Name: ______________________ Date: __________

# Activity 3B

# Literature Web

**Directions:** Complete a Literature Web for "I Hear America Singing."

**Key Words**

**Feelings**

**Ideas**

**Title**

**Images/Symbols**

**Structure**

Copyright © Kendall Hunt Publishing Company

Name: ______________________________ Date: ________________

Activity 3C

# Literature Web

**Directions:** Complete a Literature Web for "As I Grow Older."

**Key Words**

**Feelings**

**Ideas**

**Title**

**Images/Symbols**

**Structure**

Copyright © Kendall Hunt Publishing Company

# "As I Grew Older"

## Langston Hughes

It was a long time ago,
I have almost forgotten my dream.
But it was there then,
In front of me,
Bright like a sun—
My dream.

And then the wall rose,
Rose slowly,
Slowly,
Between me and my dream.
Rose until it touched the sky—
The wall.

Shadow.
I am black.

I lie down in the shadow.
No longer the light of my dream before me,
Above me.
Only the thick wall.
Only the shadow.

My hands!
My dark hands!
Break through the wall!
Find my dream!
Help me to shatter this darkness,
To smash this night,
To break this shadow
Into a thousand lights of sun,
Into a thousand whirling dreams
Of sun!

Copyright © Kendall Hunt Publishing Company

"As I Grew Older" from The Collected Poems of Langston Hughes by Langston Hughes, edited by Arnold Rampersad with David Roessel, Associate Editor, Copyright © 1994 by the Estate of Langston Hughes. Used by permission of Alfred A. Knopf, an imprint of the Knopf Doubleday Publishing Group, a division of Random House LLC. All rights reserved.

# "I Hear America Singing"

**Walt Whitman**

I hear America singing, the varied carols I hear,
Those of mechanics, each one singing his as it should
  be blithe and strong,
The carpenter singing his as he measures his plank
  or beam,
The mason singing his as he makes ready work, or
  leaves off work,
The boatman singing what belongs to him in his
  boat, the deckhand singing on the steamboat deck,
The shoemaker singing as he sits on his bench, the
  hatter singing as he stands,
The wood-cutter's song, the ploughboy's on his way
  in the morning, or at noon intermission or at sundown,
The delicious singing of the mother, or of the young
  wife at work, or of the girl sewing or washing,
Each singing what belongs to him or her and to
  no one else,
The day what belongs to the day—at night the party
  of young fellows, robust, friendly,
Singing with open mouths their strong melodious songs.

Copyright © Kendall Hunt Publishing Company

"I Hear America Singing" by Walt Whitman, 1867.

Name: ______________________________ Date: ________________

Activity 4A

# Literature Web

**Directions:** Complete a Literature Web for "Defining Liberty."

**Key Words**

**Feelings**

**Ideas**

**Title**

**Images/Symbols**

**Structure**

Copyright © Kendall Hunt Publishing Company

Name: ______________________ Date: ____________

# Activity 4B

## Vocabulary Web

**Directions:** Complete a Vocabulary Web for the word *liberty*.

**Word Families**

**Synonyms**

**Antonyms**

**Dictionary Definition**

**Word**

**Sentence in Text**

**Analysis**

**Part of Speech**

**Origin**

**Stems**

**Student Example**

Copyright © Kendall Hunt Publishing Company

Name: ______________________________ Date: ______________

Activity
4C

# *Justice* Generalizations

- What is just for one may not be just for all. (Justice is not always apparent until one is personally impacted.)
- Humans seek justice in everyday life (family, government, school, religion).
- Justice may bring benefits to large groups of people; Justice may bring overwhelming change or regression as well.
- Justice involves choice and personal decisions. Humans pursue both personal and societal justice.
- Justice may be viewed as injustice, depending upon one's perspective.

Copyright © Kendall Hunt Publishing Company

# Speech—"Defining Liberty"

### by Abraham Lincoln

## Baltimore, Maryland,

April 18, 1864

... The world has never had a good definition of the word liberty, and the American people, just now, are much in want of one. We all declare for liberty; but in using the same word we do not all mean the same thing. With some the word liberty may mean for each man to do as he pleases with himself, and the product of his labor; while with others the same word may mean for some men to do as they please with other men, and the product of other men's labor. Here are two, not only different, but incompatible things, called by the same name—liberty. And it follows that each of the things is, by the respective parties, called by two different and incompatible names—liberty and tyranny.

The shepherd drives the wolf from the sheep's throat, for which the sheep thanks the shepherd as a liberator, while the wolf denounces him for the same act as the destroyer of liberty, especially as the sheep was a black one. Plainly the sheep and the wolf are not agreed upon a definition of the word liberty; and precisely the same difference prevails today among us human creatures, even in the North, and all professing to love liberty. Hence we behold the processes by which thousands are daily passing from under the yoke of bondage, hailed by some as the advance of liberty, and bewailed by others as the destruction of all liberty. Recently, as it seems, the people of Maryland have been doing something to define liberty; and thanks to them that, in what they have done, the wolf's dictionary, has been repudiated.

A. LINCOLN

Excerpt from "Defining Liberty" by Abraham Lincoln, 1864.

Copyright © Kendall Hunt Publishing Company

Name: ________________________ Date: ____________

Activity 5A

# Literature Web

**Directions:** Complete a Literature Web for "Disappointment is the Lot of Women."

**Key Words**

**Feelings**

**Ideas**

**Title**

**Images/Symbols**

**Structure**

Copyright © Kendall Hunt Publishing Company

Name: ______________________ Date: ____________

# Activity 5B

## Vocabulary Web

**Directions:** Complete the Vocabulary Web for words from "Disappointment is the Lot of Women."

**Word Families**

**Synonyms**

**Antonyms**

**Dictionary Definition**

**Word**

**Sentence in Text**

**Analysis**

**Part of Speech**

**Origin**

**Stems**

**Student Example**

Copyright © Kendall Hunt Publishing Company

Name: ______________________________ Date: ______________

# Thoughts on Justice and Great Grammar

**Directions:** Read the quotes below. Place a vertical line between the subject and the predicate. Write the part of speech above each word. If you're unsure, see if you can figure out what the word is by examining the other parts that you do recognize.

Example:

**N. Adv. V. Adj. N. Prep. N. Adv.**

Injustice anywhere is a threat to justice everywhere.

~ Martin Luther King, Jr.

1. Unfortunately in life, justice is not always achieved.

~ Maura Tierney

2. Justice cannot be for one side alone, but must be for both.

~ Eleanor Roosevelt

3. Justice is truth in action.

~ Benjamin Disraeli

4. I think the first duty of society is justice.

~ Alexander Hamilton

Copyright © Kendall Hunt Publishing Company

# "Disappointment Is the Lot of Women"

**Lucy Stone**

The last speaker alluded to this movement as being that of a few disappointed women. From the first years to which my memory stretches, I have been a disappointed woman. When, with my brothers, I reached forth after the sources of knowledge, I was reproved with "It isn't fit for you; it doesn't belong to women." Then there was but one college in the world where women were admitted, and that was in Brazil. I would have found my way there, but by the time I was prepared to go, one was opened in the United States where women and negroes could enjoy opportunities with white men. I was disappointed when I came to seek a profession worthy of an immortal being—every employment was closed to me, except those of the teacher, the seamstress, and the housekeeper. In education, in marriage, in religion, in everything, disappointment is the lot of woman. It shall be the business of my life to deepen this disappointment in every woman's heart until she bows down to it no longer. I wish that women, instead of being walking showcases, instead of begging of their fathers and brothers the latest and gayest new bonnet, would ask of them their rights.

The question of Woman's Rights is a practical one. The notion has prevailed that it was only an ephemeral idea: that it was but women claiming the right to smoke cigars in the streets, and to frequent barrooms. Others have supposed it a question of comparative intellect; others still, of sphere. Too much has already been said and written about woman's sphere. Trace all the doctrines to their source and they will be found to have no basis except in the usages and prejudices of the age. This is seen in the fact that what

"Disappointment is the Lot of Women" by Lucy Stone, 1855.

Copyright © Kendall Hunt Publishing Company

is tolerated in woman in one country is not tolerated in another. In this country women may hold prayer-meetings, etc., but in Mohammedan countries it is written upon their mosques, "Women and dogs, and other impure animals, are not permitted to enter." Wendell Phillips says, "The best and greatest thing one is capable of doing, that is his sphere." I have confidence in the Father to believe that when He gives us the capacity to do anything He does not make a blunder. Leave women, then, to find their sphere. And do not tell us before we are born even, that our province is to cook dinners, darn stockings, and sew on buttons. We are told woman has all the rights she wants; and even women, I am ashamed to say, tell us so. They mistake the politeness of men for rights—seats while men stand in this hall tonight, and their adulations; but these are mere courtesies. We want rights. The flour-merchant, the house-builder, and the postman charge us no less on account of our sex; but when we endeavor to earn money to pay all these, then, indeed, we find the difference. Man, if he have energy, may hew out for himself a path where no mortal has ever trod, held back by nothing but what is in himself; the world is all before him, where to choose; and we are glad for you, brothers, men, that it is so. But the same society that drives forth the young man, keeps woman at home—a dependent—working little cats on worsted, and little dogs on punctured paper; but if she goes heartily and bravely to give herself to some worthy purpose, she is out of her sphere and she loses caste. Women working in tailor-shops are paid one-third as much as men. Some one in Philadelphia has stated that women make fine shirts for twelve and a half cents apiece; that no woman can make more that nine a week, and the sum thus earned, after deducting rent, fuel, etc., leaves her just three and a half cents a day for bread. Is it a wonder that women are driven to prostitution? Female teachers in New York are paid fifty dollars a year, and for every such situation there are five hundred applicants. I know not what you believe of God, but I believe He gave yearnings and longings to be filled, and that He did not mean all our time should be devoted to feeding and clothing the body. The present condition of woman causes a horrible perversion of the marriage relation. It is asked of a lady, "Has she married well?" "Oh, yes, her husband is rich." Woman must marry for a home, and you

Copyright © Kendall Hunt Publishing Company

men are the sufferers by this; for a woman who loathes you may marry you because you have the means to get money which she can not have. But when woman can enter the lists with you and make money for herself, she will marry you only for deep and earnest affection.

I am detaining you too long, many of you standing, that I ought to apologize, but women have been wronged so long that I may wrong you a little. [Applause]. A woman undertook in Lowell to sell shoes to ladies. Men laughed at her, but in six years she has run them out, and has a monopoly of the trade. Sarah Tyndale, whose husband was an importer of china, and died bankrupt, continued his business, paid off his debts, and has made a fortune and built the largest china warehouse in the world. [Mrs. Mott here corrected Lucy. Mrs. Tyndale has not the largest china warehouse, but the largest assortment of china in the world]. Mrs. Tyndale, herself, drew the plan of her warehouse, and it is the best plan ever drawn. A laborer to whom the architect showed it, said: "Don't she know e'en as much as some men?" I have seen woman at manual labor turning out chair-legs in a cabinet-shop with a dress short enough not to drag in the shavings. I wish other women would imitate her in this. It made her hands harder and broader, it is true, but I think a hand with a dollar and a quarter a day in it, better than one with crossed ninepence. The men in the shop didn't use tobacco, nor swear-they can't do those things where there are women, and we owe it to our brothers to go wherever they work to keep them decent. The widening of women's sphere is to improve her lot. Let us do it, and if the world scoff, let it scoff—if it sneer, let it sneer—but we will go emulating the example of the sisters Grimke and Abby Kelly. When they first lectured against slavery they were not listened to as respectfully as you listen to us. So the first female physician meets many difficulties, but to the next the path will be made easy.

Lucretia Mott has been a preacher for years; her right to do so is not questioned among Friends. But when Antionette Brown felt that she was commanded to preach, and to arrest the progress of thousands that were on the road to hell; why, when she applied for ordination they acted as though they had rather the whole world should go to hell, than that Antionette should be allowed to tell them how to keep out of it. She is now

Copyright © Kendall Hunt Publishing Company

ordained over a parish in the state of New York, but when she meets on the Temperance platform the Rev. John Chambers, or your own Gen Carey (applause) they greet her with hisses. Theodore Parker said; "The acorn that the school-boy carries in his pocket and the squirrel stows in his cheek, has in it the possibility of an oak, able to withstand, for ages, the cold winter and the driving blast." I have seen the acorn men and women, but never the perfect oak; all are but abortions. The young mother, when first the newborn babe nestles in her bosom, and a hertofore unknown love springs up in her heart, finds herself unprepared for this new relation in life, and she sends forth the child scarred and dwarfed by her own weakness and inbecility, as no stream can rise higher than its fountain.

Copyright © Kendall Hunt Publishing Company

# "Why Are Women Paid Less"

## Jordan Weissmann

At last night's presidential debate, audience member Katherine Fenton got up and asked how the candidates planned to fix the fact that women make "only 72 percent of what their male counterparts earn." It's a familiar stat that, as some conservatives argued today, is also a bit misleading. When you compare men and women who work similar hours in similar jobs, the gap shrinks significantly.

But it doesn't disappear. To get a sense of why women today are still paid less than men, and how much of the difference we can actually blame on discrimination, I spoke with Francine Blau, an award winning labor economist at Cornell who has published widely on gender and the workplace. Our conversation has been edited for length and clarity.

**Tell me the story of how the male-female pay gap has changed over the past few decades.**

Way back in the 1950s, women earned around 60 percent on average of what men earned when working year-round full time. And it stayed right around at that level until about 1980. Then, particularly in the decade of the 80s, there was really considerable progress in narrowing the gender pay gap. Since then, there's been further progress, but it's been a little bit more fitful, a little less consistent. So in 1980, that figure was 60 percent. In 1990 it was 72 percent. In 10 years, that was quite a change. In 2000, it was 73 percent. And now it's about 77 percent. It bounces around year to year.

**So overall, women who work full time make 77 cents for every dollar men**

© 2002 The Atlantic Media Co., as first published in The Atlantic Magazine. All rights reserved. Distributed by Tribune Content Agency, LLC.

Copyright © Kendall Hunt Publishing Company

**make. But how much of that can we actually blame on discrimination, and how much is due to other factors, like the fact that women often work in lower paying industries?**

I'm going to refer to a study with my colleague, Professor Lawrence Kahn at Cornell. In the data set we were using, women were making 20 percent less per hour than men overall. That would be what we call the unadjusted differential. As you're pointing out, this could reflect a variety of factors. It could reflect discrimination. But it also could reflect gender differences in work experience, or differences in industries and occupations. So first we statistically adjusted for human capital, which is a detailed measure of prior work experience and education. The adjusted gap was 19 percent, only slightly less than the unadjusted differential. So traditional human capital factors, taken together, do not explain that much of the gender gap. Then we have another specification, where we control for human capital but we additionally control for gender differences in industries and occupations. And that got us down to 9 percent less.

**So there was a 9 percent difference in pay you couldn't explain even when you considered the jobs women do, the education they have, or the years they spent in the workforce.**

Right.

**Is it fair to say that's a sign of discrimination at play, or what else might it be?**

On the one hand, that could be due to discrimination. On the other hand it could be due to some factors that employers know about that reflect productivity but are not possible for us to include in our analysis. So there might be gender differences—I'm not saying there are—but there might be gender differences in motivation or work commitment or negotiating skill, or a variety of unmeasured factors that we can't take into account in our analysis. On the other hand, women may be better endowed with some of the omitted factors. There's recent research suggesting interpersonal skills are becoming more important in the workplace and in general women are better endowed with those.

There's a variety of supplemental evidence that suggests there still is discrimination, even though our research suggests the amount of discrimination has decreased over the past 20 or 30 years to the extent that the unexplained gap

Copyright © Kendall Hunt Publishing Company

has decreased. David Neumark looked at waiters and waitresses in the Philadelphia area, and he actually sent testers in for the job and found that women were discriminated against in high paying restaurants. They were much less likely to accept an application from them. They were much less likely to call them back. In another one, Claudia Goldin and Cecilia Rouse did symphony orchestras. They found that when women started auditioning behind a screen, their probability of advancing increased.

Let me raise another issue for you. Nine percent could be kind of an underestimate because, how are industries and occupations determined? Employers probably have a say in what occupation and what industry people are in because they have to be hired into those jobs. So by controlling for industry and occupation, you could be controlling for some amount of discrimination. I'm not saying we are. I consider the figure that we get, controlling for industry and occupation, a relatively conservative one. Although it doesn't take away from the unmeasured factors I was talking about.

**What about the role of motherhood? How much does that really impact women's earning potential, and to what degree?**

I don't think we completely have the answer to that. But one way it does is something we were able to control for, and that is it influences how much prior work experience a person has. Because in the old days, women used to drop out of the labor force for extended periods of time when they had children, and that has changed a great deal. But that disruption certainly lowered the earnings of women compared to men, that dropping out. Now I think it's more subtle. Especially in very high level jobs, it's how much commitment can you give? Are you working 10 to 15 hours a day? It's not just a question of full time, but above and beyond, 60 hours a week. So it could be influential there. It could impact what occupations and industries women go into as well. It might make it more difficult in some that are actually higher paying.

So I think that there's no question that if we want to improve outcomes for women, we have to look at these work family issues and see how we can help accommodate balance without major detriment to either sphere. One concern I have is that some policies that are designed to help balance work and family have a

Copyright © Kendall Hunt Publishing Company

tendency to push women on to a mommy track, off the main drag.

**Can you give an example?**

I think realistically what we have now in terms of parental leave is really pretty minimal. And we could probably expand it. What we have now legislatively is 12 weeks of unpaid leave. I think it would be reasonable to pay for leave maybe on a social insurance type of basis and have it be longer, but if we make it too long, then we're sort of inviting women to step out of the labor force for a major period of time. And that's almost going back to a more traditional pattern that's going to be disruptive to them in the labor market.

**How much of the problem is just men's unwillingness to take over parenting responsibilities?**

It's kind of interesting. There has been progress. I mean, still, the women do the majority. But there has been progress. Men are putting in more time in housework and childcare. An interesting proposal that they are exploiting in some Scandinavian countries is use it or lose it parental leave for men. So in other words, parental leave in many countries, including the U.S., is available to men and women, but it's disproportionately women who take it. In these Scandinavian countries, what they've instituted is a certain amount of leave that the family only gets if the father takes it. Just traveling in Europe recently, I've seen a lot more men pushing strollers during the day.

**Mitt Romney talked a lot about workplace flexibility during the debate when asked how he would help women. What did you think of that?**

It's an issue. I think it's important to keep it in balance. President Obama certainly advocated for workplace flexibility as well, whether or not he mentioned it specifically last night. But saying it's an issue sometimes gets close to saying the only issue, and I'd like to point out that it's only partially the problem. It's not the whole problem.

**Some people point out that men and women who are unmarried and work the same number of hours earn roughly the same wages. Do you think that's a fair criticism of the idea that there really is a wage gap?**

I don't think so, because unmarried men and women are disproportionately younger. The

Copyright © Kendall Hunt Publishing Company

pay gap tends to be smaller for younger people than it is for older people. And the reasons for that, on the one hand, is discrimination. If women are having difficulty working their way up the hierarchy, that's going to show up more at older ages than it does in younger ages. On the other hand, if women have work-family issues, that can also show up more at older ages. So, just focusing on unmarried people is focusing on younger people. And so it's not, it doesn't answer the question.

**What can economists tell us about the trouble women have advancing in the workplace? Do we really know whether they get the same training or opportunities in the office?**

We certainly believe that's the case. And we do have some evidence. I've seen some studies where, even when controlling for measured factors, women will get less training than men. Mentorship has been a long-term issue, especially in male-dominated areas, or areas where the senior people are men. People still tend to identify with younger colleagues of the same sex. So they may be more supportive, encouraging and helpful to young men than they are to young women. And even how it affects women themselves. There have been some studies that suggest, for example—the evidence is a bit mixed—but one of the more interesting ones I saw, where women were randomly assigned to classes, just having a female professor in some of these scientific and technical areas increased the probability that women would go into these areas.

**If you could see just one piece of legislation on these issues passed, what would it be?**

That's a good question, but I'm not prepared to answer to it right now. We have some good anti-discrimination legislation on the books and we have to continue to enforce it. I think that some of the changes in addition to that are going to have to be voluntary changes. Employers, for example, as a larger supply of the skilled workforce that employers hire is female, they have the incentives to voluntarily address these work family issues. And they are. It's still not enough, but they increasingly are doing so. So we need a sort of combined approach of government and the private sector.

Copyright © Kendall Hunt Publishing Company

Name: ______________________ Date: ______________

Activity 6A

# Literature Web

**Directions:** Complete a Literature Web about the article "Will a Longer School Year Help or Hurt U.S. Students?".

**Key Words**

**Feelings**

**Ideas**

**Title**

**Images/Symbols**

**Structure**

Copyright © Kendall Hunt Publishing Company

Name: ______________________ Date: ____________

# Activity 6B

## Vocabulary Web

**Directions:** Complete a Vocabulary Web about a new or interesting word from the article "Will a Longer School Year Help or Hurt U.S. Students?".

**Word Families**

**Synonyms**

**Antonyms**

**Dictionary Definition**

**Word**

**Sentence in Text**

**Analysis**

**Part of Speech**

**Origin**

**Stems**

**Student Example**

Copyright © Kendall Hunt Publishing Company

Name: ______________________________ Date: ______________

# Elements of Reasoning

**Directions:** Review these *Elements of Reasoning*. These elements can help you to think and argue better. Try to incorporate them in your writing.

1. Purpose or Goal

2. Issue or Problem

3. Point of View

4. Experiences, Data, or Evidence

5. Concepts or Ideas

6. Assumptions

7. Inferences

8. Implications and Consequences

Copyright © Kendall Hunt Publishing Company

Name: ______________________________ Date: ______________

**Activity 6D**

# Reasoning About a Situation or Event

**Directions:** Take notes responding to each question.

What Is the Situation?

Who are the stakeholders for this situation?

What is the point of view for each stakeholder?

What are the assumptions of each group?

What are the implications of these views?

Copyright © Kendall Hunt Publishing Company

# "Will a Longer School Year Help or Hurt U.S. Students?"

**Billy Hallowell**

**Did your kids** moan that winter break was way too short as you got them ready for the first day back in school? They might get their wish of more holiday time off under proposals catching on around the country to lengthen the school year.

But it won't be entirely palatable, as there's a catch: a much shorter summer vacation.

Education Secretary Arne Duncan, a chief proponent of the longer school year, says American students have fallen behind the world academically.

"Whether educators have more time to enrich instruction or students have more time to learn how to play an instrument and write computer code, adding meaningful in-school hours is a critical investment that better prepares children to be successful in the 21st century," he said in December when five states announced they would add at least 300 hours to the academic calendar in some schools beginning this year.

The three-year pilot project will affect about 20,000 students in 40 schools in Colorado, Connecticut, Massachusetts, New York and Tennessee.

Proponents argue that too much knowledge is lost while American kids wile away the summer months apart from their lessons. The National Summer Learning Association cites decades of research that shows students' test scores are higher in the same subjects at the beginning of the summer than at the end.

"The research is very clear about that," said Charles Ballinger, executive director emeritus of the National Association for Year-

Copyright © 2013 The Associated Press. Reprinted by permission.

Copyright © Kendall Hunt Publishing Company

Round Education in San Diego. "The only ones who don't lose are the upper 10 to 15 percent of the student body. Those tend to be gifted, college-bound, they're natural learners who will learn wherever they are."

Supporters also say a longer school year would give poor children more access to school-provided healthy meals.

Yet the movement has plenty of detractors—so many that Ballinger sometimes feels like the Grinch trying to steal Christmas.

"I had a parent at one meeting say, 'I want my child to lie on his back in the grass watching the clouds in the sky during the day and the moon and stars at night,'" Ballinger recalled. "I thought, 'Oh, my. Most kids do that for two, three, maybe four days, then say, 'What's next?'""

But opponents aren't simply dreamy romantics.

Besides the outdoor opportunities for pent up youngsters, they say families already are beholden to the school calendar for three seasons out of four. Summer breaks, they say, are needed to provide an academic respite for students' overwrought minds, and to provide time with family and the flexibility to travel and study favorite subjects in more depth. They note that advocates of year-round school cannot point to any evidence that it brings appreciable academic benefits.

"I do believe that if children have not mastered a subject that, within a week, personally, I see a slide in my own child," said Tina Bruno, executive director of the Coalition for a Traditional School Calendar. "That's where the idea of parental involvement and parental responsibility in education comes in, because our children cannot and should not be in school seven days a week, 365 days a year."

Bruno is part of a "Save Our Summers" alliance of parents, grandparents, educational professionals and some summer-time recreation providers fighting year-round school. Local chapters carry names such as Georgians Need Summers, Texans for a Traditional School Year and Save Alabama Summers.

Camps, hotel operators and other summer-specific industries raise red flags about the potential economic effect.

The debate has divided parents and educators.

School days shorter than work days and summer breaks that extend to as many as 12 weeks in some areas run up against increasing political pressure from working households—30 percent of which are headed by women.

Copyright © Kendall Hunt Publishing Company

These families must fill the gaps with afterschool programs, day care, babysitters and camps.

"Particularly where there are single parents or where both parents are working, they prefer to provide care for three weeks at a time rather than three months at a time," Ballinger said.

The National Center on Time & Learning has estimated that about 1,000 districts have adopted longer school days or years.

Some places that have tried the year-round calendar, including Salt Lake City, Las Vegas and parts of California, have returned to the traditional approach. Strapped budgets and parental dissatisfaction were among reasons.

School years are extended based on three basic models:

- stretching the traditional 180 days of school across the whole calendar year by lengthening spring and winter breaks and shortening the one in the summer.
- adding 20 to 30 actual days of instruction to the 180-day calendar.
- dividing students and staff into groups, typically four, and rotating three through at a time, with one on vacation, throughout the calendar year.

At the heart of the debate is nothing less than the ability of America's workforce to compete globally.

The U.S. remains in the top dozen or so countries in all tested subjects. But even where U.S. student scores have improved, many other nations have improved much faster, leaving American students far behind peers in Asia and Europe.

Still, data are far from clear that more hours behind a desk can help.

A Center for Public Education review found that students in India and China—countries Duncan has pointed to as giving children more classroom time than the U.S.—don't actually spend more time in school than American kids, when disparate data are converted to apples-to-apples comparisons.

The center, an initiative of the National School Boards Association, found 42 U.S. states require more than 800 instructional hours a year for their youngest students, and that's more than India does.

Opponents of extended school point out that states such as Minnesota and Massachusetts steadily shine on standardized achievement tests while preserving their summer break with a post-Labor Day school start.

"It makes sense that more time is going to equate to more learning, but then you have to equate that to more professional development

Copyright © Kendall Hunt Publishing Company

for teachers—will that get more bang for the buck?" said Patte Barth, the center's director. "I look at it, and teachers and instruction are still the most important factor more so than time."

The center's study also found that some nations that outperform the U.S. academically, such as Finland, require less school.

Many schools are experimenting with the less controversial, less costly interim step of lengthening the school day instead of adding days to the school year.

Chicago's public schools extended the school day from 5 hours and 45 minutes to 7 hours last year after a heated offensive by unionized teachers and some parents. Mayor Rahm Emanuel, former chief of staff to Duncan's boss, President Barack Obama, initially pushed an even longer school day—a major sticking point in this year's seven-day teachers' strike. He and other proponents argued that having the shortest school day among the nation's 50 largest districts and one of the shortest school years had put Chicago's children at a competitive disadvantage.

Wendy Katten, executive director of Raise Your Hand for Illinois Public Education, said opponents held back a push for a 7.5-hour school day, and got an extra staff person assigned to each school to handle the additional hour and 15 minutes of school time.

In San Diego, year-round school has been a reality since the 1970s.

District spokesman Jack Brandais said the concept was initially intended to relieve crowding, not improve performance test scores. The student body and staff were divided into four groups, with three attending school at any given time.

Through decades of fine-tuning, Brandais said the district now runs both traditional and year-round tracks simultaneously.

A 2007 study by Ohio State University sociologist Paul von Hippel found virtually no difference in the academic gains of students who followed a traditional nine-month school calendar and those educated the same number of days spread across the entire year.

Amid budget cuts and teacher layoffs, San Diego has cut five instructional days from both year-round and traditional schedules since last year.

Copyright © Kendall Hunt Publishing Company

Name: ______________________________ Date: ______________

# Vocabulary Web

**Directions:** Complete a Vocabulary Web for the word *humble.*

**Word Families**

**Synonyms**

**Antonyms**

**Dictionary Definition**

**Word**

**Sentence in Text**

**Analysis**

**Part of Speech**

**Origin**

**Stems**

**Student Example**

Copyright © Kendall Hunt Publishing Company

Name: ______________________________ Date: ______________

# Activity 7B Vocabulary from "The Valiant Chattee Maker"

**Directions:** Review the vocabulary from the novel as directed by your teacher.

1. banyan tree
2. bellicose
3. blunder
4. confiscate
5. decrepit
6. docile
7. eke
8. formidable
9. intrepid
10. perpetual
11. Rajah/Maharajah
12. reconnaissance
13. resplendent
14. rogue
15. vex

Copyright © Kendall Hunt Publishing Company

Name: ______________________ Date: ______________

Activity 7C

# Vocabulary Web

**Directions:** Complete a Vocabulary Web for a word from "The Valiant Chattee Maker."

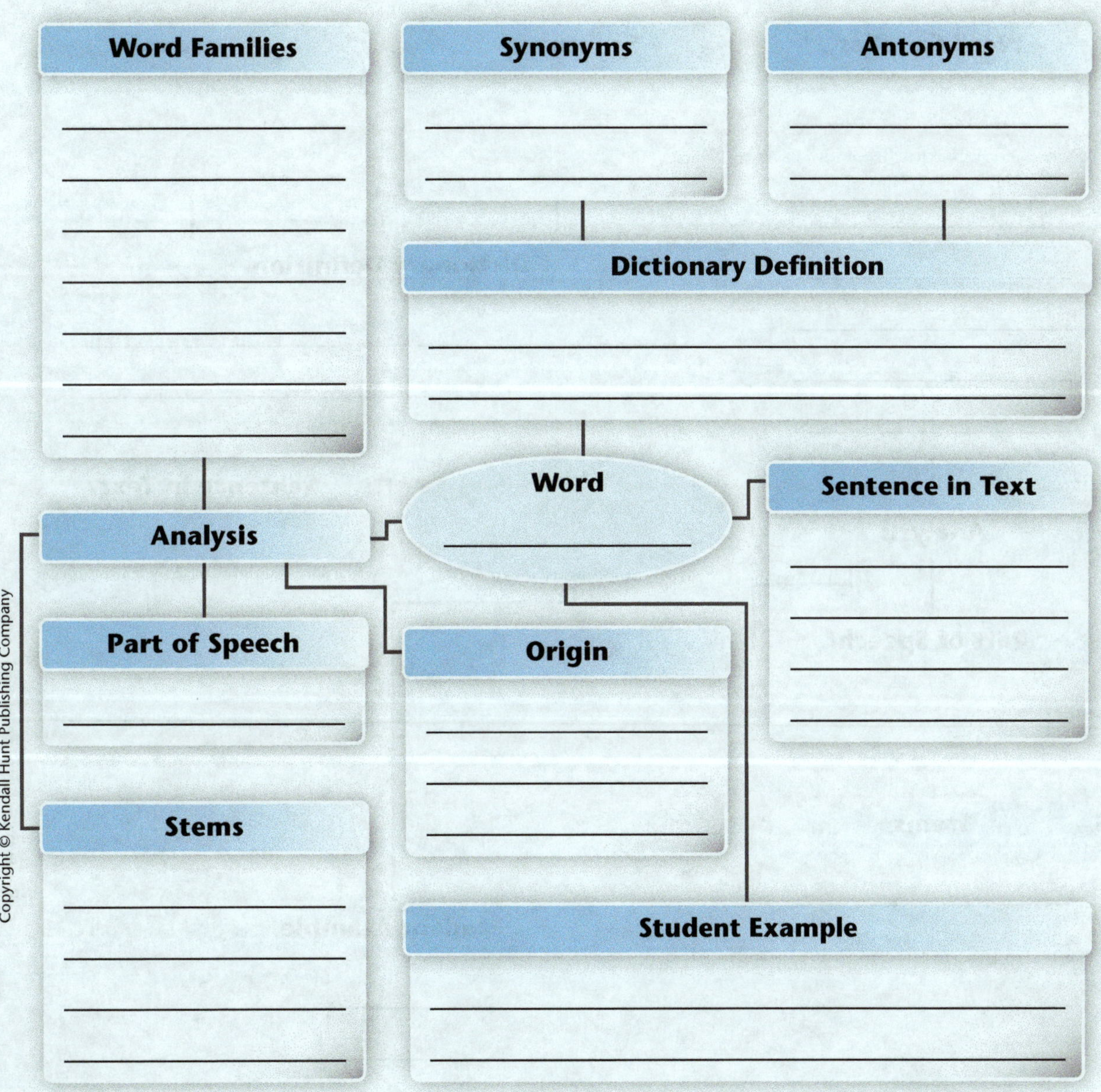


Copyright © Kendall Hunt Publishing Company

Name: ______________________ Date: ______________

# Activity 7D

## Vocabulary Web

**Directions:** Complete a Vocabulary Web for a word from "The Valiant Chattee Maker."

**Word Families**

**Synonyms**

**Antonyms**

**Dictionary Definition**

**Word**

**Sentence in Text**

**Analysis**

**Part of Speech**

**Origin**

**Stems**

**Student Example**

Copyright © Kendall Hunt Publishing Company

Name: ______________________________ Date: ________________

# Literature Web

**Directions:** Complete a Literature Web for "The Valiant Chattee Maker."

**Key Words**

______________________

______________________

______________________

______________________

______________________

**Feelings**

______________________

______________________

______________________

______________________

______________________

**Ideas**

______________________

______________________

______________________

______________________

______________________

______________________

______________________

______________________

**Title**

______________________

______________________

______________________

______________________

**Images/Symbols**

______________________

______________________

______________________

______________________

______________________

______________________

______________________

______________________

**Structure**

______________________________________________

______________________________________________

______________________________________________

______________________________________________

Copyright © Kendall Hunt Publishing Company

# "The Valiant Chattee Maker"

Long, long ago, in a violent storm of thunder, lightning, wind, and rain, a tiger crept for shelter close to the wall of an old woman's hut. This old woman was very poor, and her hut was but a tumble-down place, through the roof of which the rain came drip, drip, drip, on more sides than one. This troubled her much, and she went running about from side to side, dragging first one thing and then another out of the way of the leaky places in the roof, and as she did so, she kept saying to herself, "Oh dear! Oh dear! How tiresome this is! I'm sure the roof will come down! If an elephant, or a lion, or a tiger were to walk in, he wouldn't frighten me half as much as this perpetual dripping." And then she would begin dragging the bed and all the other things in the room about again, to get them out of the way of the rain. The Tiger, who was crouching down just outside, heard all that she said, and thought to himself, "This old woman says she would not be afraid of an elephant, or a lion, or a tiger, but that this perpetual dripping frightens her more than all. What can this 'perpetual dripping' be? It must be something very dreadful." And, hearing her immediately afterwards dragging all the things about the room again, he said to himself, "What a terrible noise! Surely that must be the '*perpetual dripping*.'"

At this moment a Chattee-maker,[1] who was in search of his donkey which had strayed away, came down the road. The night being very cold, he had, truth to say, taken a little more toddy[2] than was good for him, and seeing, by the light of a flash of lightning, a large animal lying down close to the old woman's hut, mistook it for the donkey he was looking for.

Copyright © Kendall Hunt Publishing Company

[1] Potter.

[2] An intoxicating drink made of palm juice.

From Eastern Fairy Legends: Current in Southern India by Mary Frere. Copyright © 1847 by J.B. Lippincott & Co.

So, running up to the Tiger, he seized hold of it by one ear, and commenced beating, kicking, and abusing it with all his might and main.

"You wretched creature," he cried, "is this the way you serve me, obliging me to come out and look for you in such pouring rain, and on such a dark night as this? Get up instantly, or I'll break every bone in your body;" and he went on scolding and thumping the Tiger with his utmost power, for he had worked himself up into a terrible rage. The Tiger did not know what to make of it all, but he began to feel quite frightened, and said to himself, "Why, this must be the 'perpetual dripping'; no wonder the old woman said she was more afraid of it than of an elephant, a lion, or a tiger, for it gives most dreadfully hard blows."

The Chattee-maker, having made the Tiger get up, got on his back, and forced him to carry him home, kicking and beating him the whole way (for all this time he fancied he was on his donkey), and then he tied his fore feet and his head firmly together, and fastened him to a post in front of his house, and when he had done this he went to bed.

Next morning, when the Chattee-maker's wife got up and looked out of the window, what did she see but a great big Tiger tied up in front of their house, to the post to which they usually fastened the donkey; she was very much surprised, and running to her husband, awoke him, saying, "Do you know what animal you fetched home last night?" "Yes, the donkey, to be sure," he answered. "Come and see," said she, and she showed him the great Tiger tied to the post. The Chattee-maker at this was no less astonished than his wife, and felt himself all over to find out if the Tiger had not wounded him. But no there he was, safe and sound, and there was the Tiger tied to the post, just as he had fastened it up the night before.

News of the Chattee-maker's exploit soon spread through the village, and all the people came to see him and hear him tell how he had caught the Tiger and tied it to the post; and this they thought so wonderful, that they sent a deputation to the Rajah, with a letter to tell him how a man of their village had, alone and unarmed, caught a great Tiger, and tied it to a post.

When the Rajah read the letter he also was much surprised, and determined to go in person and see this astonishing sight. So he sent for his horses and carriages, his lords and attendants, and they

Copyright © Kendall Hunt Publishing Company

all set off together to look at the Chattee-maker and the Tiger he had caught.

Now the Tiger was a very large one, and had long been the terror of all the country round, which made the whole matter still more extraordinary; and this being represented to the Rajah, he determined to confer every possible honour on the valiant Chattee-maker. So he gave him houses and lands, and as much money as would fill a well, made him lord of his court, and conferred on him the command of ten thousand horse.

It came to pass, shortly after this, that a neighbouring Rajah, who had long had a quarrel with this one, sent to announce his intention of going instantly to war with him; and tidings were at the same time brought that the Rajah who sent the challenge had gathered a great army together on the borders, and was prepared at a moment's notice to invade the country.

In this dilemma no one knew what to do. The Rajah sent for all his generals, and inquired which of them would be willing to take command of his forces and oppose the enemy. They all replied that the country was so ill-prepared for the emergency, and the case was apparently so hopeless, that they would rather not take the responsibility of the chief command. The Rajah knew not whom to appoint in their stead. Then some of his people said to him, "You have lately given command of ten thousand horse to the valiant Chattee-maker who caught the Tiger, why not make him Commander-in-Chief? A man who could catch a Tiger and tie him to a post must surely be more courageous and clever than most." "Very well," said the Rajah, "I will make him Commander-in-Chief." So he sent for the Chattee-maker and said to him, "In your hands I place all the power of the kingdom; you must put our enemies to flight." "So be it," answered the Chattee-maker, "but, before I lead the whole army against the enemy, suffer me to go by myself and examine their position; and, if possible, find out their numbers and strength."

The Rajah consented, and the Chattee-maker returned home to his wife, and said, "They have made me Commander-in-Chief which is a very difficult post for me to fill, because I shall have to ride at the head of all the army, and you know I never was on a horse in my life. But I have succeeded in gaining a little delay, as the Rajah has given me permission to go first alone, and reconnoitre the

Copyright © Kendall Hunt Publishing Company

enemy's camp. Do you, therefore, provide a very quiet pony, for you know I cannot ride, and I will start to-morrow morning."

But before the Chattee-maker had started, the Rajah sent over to him a most magnificent charger, richly caparisoned, which he begged he would ride when going to see the enemy's camp. The Chattee-maker was frightened almost out of his life, for the charger that the Rajah had sent him was very powerful and spirited, and he felt sure that, even if he ever got on it, he should very soon tumble off; however, he did not dare to refuse it, for fear of offending the Rajah by not accepting his present. So he sent him back a message of dutiful thanks, and said to his wife, "I cannot go on the pony now that the Rajah has sent me this fine horse, but how am I ever to ride it?" "Oh, don't be frightened," she answered, "you've only got to get upon it, and I will tie you firmly on, so that you cannot tumble off, and if you start at night no one will see that you are tied on." "Very well," he said. So that night his wife brought the horse that the Rajah had sent him to the door. "Indeed," said the Chattee-maker, "I can never get into that saddle, it is so high up." "You must jump," said his wife. Then he tried to jump several times, but each time he jumped he tumbled down again. "I always forget when I am jumping," said he, "which way I ought to turn." "Your face must be towards the horse's head," she answered. "To be sure, of course," he cried, and giving one great jump he jumped into the saddle, but with his face towards the horse's tail. "This won't do at all," said his wife as she helped him down again; "try getting on without jumping." "I never can remember," he continued, "when I have got my left foot in the stirrup, what to do with my right foot, or where to put it." "That must go in the other stirrup," she answered; "let me help you." So, after many trials, in which he tumbled down very often, for the horse was fresh and did not like standing still, the Chattee-maker got into the saddle; but no sooner had he got there than he cried, "O wife, wife! Tie me very firmly as quickly as possible, for I know I shall jump down if I can." Then she fetched some strong rope and tied his feet firmly into the stirrups, and fastened one stirrup to the other, and put another rope round his waist, and another round his neck, and fastened them to the horse's body, and neck, and tail.

When the horse felt all these ropes about him he could not

Copyright © Kendall Hunt Publishing Company

imagine what queer creature had got upon his back, and he began rearing, and kicking, and prancing, and at last set off full gallop, as fast as he could tear, right across country. "Wife, wife," cried the Chattee-maker, "you forgot to tie my hands." "Never mind," said she; "hold on by the mane." So he caught hold of the horse's mane as firmly as he could. Then away went horse, away went Chattee-maker, away, away, away, over hedges, over ditches, over rivers, over plains, away, away, like a flash of lightning, now this way, now that, on, on, on, gallop, gallop, gallop, until they came in sight of the enemy's camp.

The Chattee-maker did not like his ride at all, and when he saw where it was leading him he liked it still less, for he thought the enemy would catch him and very likely kill him. So he determined to make one desperate effort to be free, and stretching out his hand as the horse shot past a young banyan-tree, seized hold of it with all his might, hoping the resistance it offered might cause the ropes that tied him to break. But the horse was going at his utmost speed, and the soil in which the banyan-tree grew was loose, so that when the Chattee-maker caught hold of it and gave it such a violent pull, it came up by the roots, and on he rode as fast as before, with the tree in his hand.

All the soldiers in the camp saw him coming, and having heard that an army was to be sent against them, made sure that the Chattee-maker was one of the vanguard. "See," cried they, "here comes a man of gigantic stature on a mighty horse! He rides at full speed across the country, tearing up the very trees in his rage! He is one of the opposing force; the whole army must be close at hand. If they are such as he, we are all dead men." Then, running to their Rajah, some of them cried again, "Here comes the whole force of the enemy" (for the story had by this time become exaggerated); "they are men of gigantic stature, mounted on mighty horses; as they come they tear up the very trees in their rage; we can oppose men, but not monsters such as these." These were followed by others, who said, "It is all true," for by this time the Chattee-maker had got pretty near the camp, "they're coming! They're coming! Let us fly! Let us fly! Fly, fly for your lives!" And the whole panic stricken multitude fled from the camp (those who had seen no cause for alarm going because the others did, or because they did not care to stay by themselves) after having obliged their Rajah to write

Copyright © Kendall Hunt Publishing Company

a letter to the one whose country he was about to invade, to say that he would not do so, and propose terms of peace, and to sign it, and seal it with his seal. Scarcely had all the people fled from the camp, when the horse on which the Chattee-maker was came galloping into it, and on his back rode the Chattee-maker, almost dead from fatigue, with the banyan-tree in his hand. Just as he reached the camp the ropes by which he was tied broke, and he fell to the ground. The horse stood still, too tired with its long run to go further. On recovering his senses, the Chattee-maker discovered, to his surprise, that the whole camp, full of rich arms, clothes, and trappings, was entirely deserted. In the principal tent, moreover, he found a letter addressed to his Rajah, announcing the retreat of the invading army, and proposing terms of peace.

So he took the letter, and returned home with it as fast as he could, leading his horse all the way, for he was afraid to mount him again. It did not take him long to reach his house by the direct road, for whilst riding he had gone a more circuitous journey than was necessary, and he got there just at nightfall. His wife ran out to meet him, overjoyed at his speedy return. As soon as he saw her, he said, "Ah, wife, since I saw you last I've been all round the world, and had many wonderful and terrible adventures. But never mind that now, send this letter quickly to the Rajah by a messenger, and also the horse that he sent for me to ride. He will then see, by the horse looking so tired, what a long ride I've had, and if he is sent on beforehand, I shall not be obliged to ride him up to the palace-door to-morrow morning, as I otherwise should, and that would be very tiresome, for most likely I should tumble off." So his wife sent the horse and the letter to the Rajah, and a message that her husband would be at the palace early next morning, as it was then late at night. And next day he went down there as he had said he would, and when the people saw him coming, they said, "This man is as modest as he is brave; after having put our enemies to flight, he walks quite simply to the door, instead of riding here in state; as any other man would."

Copyright © Kendall Hunt Publishing Company

Name: ______________________ Date: ______________

# Step 1: Understanding Your Research Assignment

Many times you receive so much information in one large stack of papers or lecture that you cannot possibly digest the information at one time. This is a handbook designed to help you break the research process into manageable parts. It can be used as a reference to check that you have completed each stage of your project.

## Understanding the Assignment

**Directions:** Answer each of the following questions in order to make sure you understand the assignment. Make notes about any additional questions you have or other information you need to clarify.

- *What is the general topic and scope of the assignment?*
- *Will the research product be informational? Will it present different perspectives about a topic? Will it present one side of a topic with multiple perspectives? Will it be argumentative or persuasive?*
- *How many sources will I need? What types? Is there a limit on any type of source?*
- *What is the final product format (paper, multimedia, poster, oral presentation, etc.)?*
- *How long should the written portion of the research be? Is there a minimum and maximum number of pages?*
- *What does the timeline for this entire product look like? When is each part due?*

Copyright © Kendall Hunt Publishing Company

Name: ______________________ Date: ____________

# Activity 8B

# Step 2: Determining an Issue to Research

**Directions:** Complete the following tasks to help you determine an issue for your research.

## 1. Choosing an Issue

After you have done a bit of preliminary thinking or have considered possible issue ideas, ask yourself some questions to help narrow your issue to something that you can research in the timeframe allotted:

- ***Is this issue pertinent to students your age?***
  Consider researching an issue that students your age are concerned about in a significant way. What matters to your peers?
- ***Is this issue one that is rich with information that can be found and used? Can you find enough information about it?***
  Do not try to research "children who have written a novel that has received the Newbery Award" if none exists.
- ***Is your issue focused or narrow enough for the assignment? Can the issue be narrowed down to an issue or view that allows you to meet the assignment's requirements?***
  Beware of choosing an issue like "American Healthcare Reform" for a two-page paper. This is an example of an issue that is far too broad.

Copyright © Kendall Hunt Publishing Company

8B Step 2: Determining an Issue to Research (Continued)

## 2. Brainstorming Issues

A. Brainstorm a list of at least five focused issues within your broader issue that interest you and that fit the assignment's requirements. List them here:

1. ______________________________

2. ______________________________

3. ______________________________

4. ______________________________

5. ______________________________

B. If you find listing issues to be a challenge, use a web or graphic organizer. You can use technology to do this or draw it out by hand.

C. Review the more focused issues you have listed. Think about each. Examine your assignment and how long you will be working with this issue. Now, consider which issue interests you most and list it:

______________________________

Copyright © Kendall Hunt Publishing Company

Name: ______________________ Date: ______________

Activity 8C

# Step 3A: Preliminary Research

**Directions:** Read this information and complete the following tasks to assist in your research.

## 1. Finding Sources That Fit

For sources, you may find yourself drawn more to one type of source than another. For example, you may have only used a book, the Internet, or a magazine to find information. A myriad of sources is at your fingertips and in your library media center; however, some types of sources may be better than others for your particular issue. For example, if a friend asked you who won the election last night, you would not look in a novel written five years ago. You want to use the appropriate source in the correct way.

***Places to start:***

- School media center or local library: Books, magazines, newspapers, reference books/materials
- School, city/county, or university reference librarian or media specialist: Specialized collections or reference materials
- Google, Bing, Kayak, Yahoo or other search engine: Searches for specific information
- An expert in the field you are going to research: Information about topic from the perspective of someone who works in the discipline of interest

Copyright © Kendall Hunt Publishing Company

8C Step 3A: Preliminary Research (Continued)

## 2. Brainstorming Possible Sources

Think again about the assignment and the more focused issue you think will work for it. List some types of sources that are likely to be the most useful for learning about your topic. Remember, you can always decide to add to the types of sources to use along the way.

1. ________________________________________________

2. ________________________________________________

3. ________________________________________________

4. ________________________________________________

5. ________________________________________________

Copyright © Kendall Hunt Publishing Company

Name: ______________________________ Date: ______________

# Activity 8D

# Step 3B: Preliminary Research

**Directions:** Read the following information and respond to the questions as you start to find sources.

## A. Finding Sources

Once you have some of your sources, you are not quite ready to start your reading or taking your notes yet. Instead, conduct a critical review to see if the sources will work for your product. Use the following questions to determine the usefulness of the sources:

1. *Do you have enough or more than the required number and type of sources?*

_______________________________________________

_______________________________________________

2. *Are the authors of your sources experts in their fields? (Websites may take a bit more work to learn about the authors or the reliability of the source.)*

_______________________________________________

_______________________________________________

3. *Are your sources current? (Check with your teacher to determine if sources must have been published within a certain time period.)*

_______________________________________________

_______________________________________________

Copyright © Kendall Hunt Publishing Company

**8D** **Step 3B: Preliminary Research (Continued)**

**4.** *Are your sources written at an appropriate level for you and your assignment?*

**5.** *Are your sources too broad or too vague?*

**6.** *Is the information verifiable?*

**7.** *Are facts and opinions clearly distinguishable?*

**8.** *Are charts, maps, interviews, or other aspects of the sources reliable, factual, current, and helpful to your type of research?*

Copyright © Kendall Hunt Publishing Company

## B. A Quick Checklist for Evaluating Sources for Your Research Paper

***Always Keep in Mind:***

Just because someone wrote a book (article, editorial, etc.) or set up a website does not mean that all information contained therein is reliable or valuable for your research product. There is no standard or screening agency available to ensure that all of the information is accurate. To help you examine a resource, think of the following as filters that can help you examine the worthiness of a source for your particular product:

**Accuracy:** Free from errors

**Breadth:** Encompassing multiple viewpoints

**Fairness:** Justifiable; not one-sided

**Current:** The timeliness of the information

**Significance:** Focusing on the important aspects of the issue

**Relevance:** Relating to the issue being researched

You should apply these filters as criteria as you examine and read sources. A good source meeting all of these criteria will be of the most use to you.

Copyright © Kendall Hunt Publishing Company

Name: ______________________ Date: ______________

# Step 3C: More Preliminary Research

**Activity 8E**

**Directions:** Complete the following exercises to help you focus your issue.

## 1. Digging into Your Research

Your More Focused Issue: ______________________

List three or four (or more) probing questions about your issue:

A. ______________________

B. ______________________

C. ______________________

D. ______________________

## 2. Focusing Your Issue

Review your issue again and the questions you have written. What do you think the focus of your paper will be based on these?

______________________

Think of one overarching question that you will be answering. This may change as you read and research, but thinking about it and writing it down now will enable you to be specific in how you now approach the sources for information to be gathered.

______________________

______________________

______________________

Copyright © Kendall Hunt Publishing Company

Name: ______________________________ Date: ______________

# Step 3D: Preliminary Research: A Note About Plagiarism

**Directions:** Please read the following information about plagiarism.

Your integrity matters. You need to learn how to research, write, cite properly, and avoid any hint of plagiarism. Plagiarism is a serious academic offense.

When you take someone else's ideas, thoughts, way with words, music, images, etc. without acknowledging that person or group (through citations), you have committed plagiarism.

Plagiarism can be:

- Copying sentences, phrases or paragraphs exactly as they appear in the original source
- Copying sentences and putting them in a different order
- Copying sentences and replacing a few words with synonyms
- Copying sentences and adding a few of your own

(Source of this four point list is the Penn State University Library online at http://www.libraries.psu.edu/psul/lls/students/plagiarism_and_you.html)

## Citing Sources

Citing your sources may sound intimidating, but it simply means you are telling anyone reading your paper where the ideas originated. You are giving them the intellectual respect deserved when you properly cite your sources.

Copyright © Kendall Hunt Publishing Company

**8F** **Step 3D: Preliminary Research: A Note About Plagiarism (Continued)**

*If these ideas are difficult, seeing examples may help. Learn more about the types of plagiarism and read examples at Plagiarism.org online. The Online Writing Lab at Purdue has information about ways to paraphrase, cite sources, and avoid plagiarism. They also have some exercises you can do in order to become better at paraphrasing or knowing what is and is not plagiarism. OWL's site is https://owl.english.purdue.edu/owl/resource/589/01/*

*Another site, http://www.geneseo.edu/~brainard/plagiarismtypes.htm also has some examples to peruse.*

Copyright © Kendall Hunt Publishing Company

Name: ______________________ Date: ____________

Activity 8G

# Step 3E: Preliminary Research: Learning to Say What You Learned and Avoiding Plagiarism

**Directions:** Read the following information. Keep this page available as you conduct your research.

From Purdue University's Online Writing Lab (OWL) at http://owl.english.purdue.edu/owl/resource/589/2/

**A brief list of what needs to be credited or documented:**

- Words or ideas presented in a magazine, book, newspaper, song, TV program, movie, Web page, computer program, letter, advertisement, or any other medium
- Information you gain through interviewing or conversing with another person, face to face, over the phone, or in writing
- When you copy the exact words or a unique phrase
- When you reprint any diagrams, illustrations, charts, pictures, or other visual materials
- When you reuse or repost any available media, including images, audio, video, or other media from any source online, in a text, etc.

*Bottom line, document any words, ideas, or other productions that originate somewhere outside of you.*

**There are, of course, certain things that do not need documentation or credit, including:**

- Writing your own life experiences; your own thoughts, observations and insights; your own thoughts; and your own conclusions about a subject
- When you are writing up your own results obtained through lab or field experiments

Copyright © Kendall Hunt Publishing Company

8G **Step 3E: Preliminary Research: Learning to Say What You Learned and Avoiding Plagiarism (Continued)**

- When you use your own artwork, digital photographs, video, audio, etc.
- When you are using "common knowledge," things like folklore, common sense observations, myths, urban legends, and historical events (but not historical documents)
- When you are using generally-accepted facts, e.g., pollution is bad for the environment, including facts that are accepted within particular discourse communities, e.g., in the field of composition studies, "writing is a process" is a generally-accepted fact.

## Deciding if Something is "Common Knowledge"

This may be a new idea. Generally speaking, you can regard something as common knowledge if you find the same information undocumented in at least five credible texts or sources. Additionally, it might be common knowledge if you think the information you're presenting is something your readers will already know, or something that a person could easily find in general reference sources. But if you have any question or you are in doubt, cite; if the citation turns out to be unnecessary, your teacher or editor will tell you. You must, of course, document all direct quotations. You must also document any ideas borrowed from a source: paraphrases of sentences, summaries of paragraphs or chapters, statistics or little-known facts, and tables, graphs, or diagrams.

Copyright © Kendall Hunt Publishing Company

Name: ______________________________ Date: ______________

Activity 8H

# Step 3F: Even More Preliminary Research

**Directions:** Use the following guide to help you maintain a list of possible sources for your research.

## Researching Print Sources

Look at your print sources: books, magazine articles, journals, etc. You will save a great deal of time by organizing your approach to these texts. Think of the following questions to guide how you approach your print sources:

**A.** *Is your topic listed in the table of contents? The index? Chapter titles? If so, how is it worded as a listing? To prepare to take notes, on a sticky note, write down the words or phrases that the author uses to describe your topic and the page numbers where your topic can be found. By using a sticky note, you can easily place it in the text and read the entire part or section later, but you will not have to try to recall which book or magazine from which a particular fact came.*

**B.** *What about any related topics or subtopics that are listed when you find yours in the table of contents, index, etc.? These might help you find additional evidence for your paper.*

You can use a chart like the one on the next page to keep track of which sources you want to use. You can make a hard copy, keep it in a Word document, an Excel spreadsheet, or electronic sticky notes, etc. The point is to document the sources you are using. (Remember, you may have sources that seemed to have potential, but upon further inspection, they do not meet your needs. It is okay to discard some or add more as you begin your paper. It is much better to have a source and not need it than it is to try to find one and discover that no others exist that fit your topic.)

Copyright © Kendall Hunt Publishing Company

**8H** **Step 3F: Even More Preliminary Research (Continued)**

| | Author | Title | Word/Phrase Listing | Page(s) |
|---|---|---|---|---|
| 1. | | | | |
| 2. | | | | |
| 3. | | | | |
| 4. | | | | |
| 5. | | | | |
| 6. | | | | |
| 7. | | | | |
| 8. | | | | |
| 9. | | | | |
| 10. | | | | |

Copyright © Kendall Hunt Publishing Company

Name: ______________________________ Date: ______________

# Activity 81

## Step 3G: Preliminary Research

**Directions:** Use the following guide to assist you in your research.

### Researching Internet Sources

- Remember, a background knowledge base is a good place to start. Reading through an Internet encyclopedia may give you some background information or list some great resources to search in its Bibliography or Works Cited section. However, many teachers will not allow you to use such a resource as a source to be internally cited in your final piece.
- You have to have a place to start, determine your position, and gather resources to support you. You may also need to find one or two pieces that give you that general knowledge.
- Please do NOT ever list Wikipedia as a source, resource, or citation. You are free to read it or look at its bibliography. It is not considered a reliable site to cite, since it is a wiki and can be edited by anyone.

### Your Plan of Attack for Internet Sources

- Look at the list of keywords or phrases that you found when you were looking at print materials. Use a search engine to find three to five (or more) sites.
- To help you examine a source, think of the following as filters that can help you examine the worthiness of a source for your particular product:
    - **Accuracy:** Free from errors
    - **Breadth:** Encompassing multiple viewpoints
    - **Fairness:** Justifiable; not one-sided
    - **Current:** The timeliness of the information
    - **Significance:** Focusing on the important aspects of the issue
    - **Relevance:** Relating to the issue being researched

Copyright © Kendall Hunt Publishing Company

81 **Step 3G: Preliminary Research (Continued)**

You should apply these filters as criteria as you examine and read sources. A good source meets all of these criteria to be of the most use to you.

List the most promising sites by the name of the site and the web address.

| **Name of Website** | **Address of Website** |
|---|---|
| 1. | |
| 2. | |
| 3. | |
| 4. | |
| 5. | |

You may wish to bookmark these sites as future resources that you can read later. Delicious is a social bookmarking site that may be used individually or with a group, so you may want to set that up for your use.

Copyright © Kendall Hunt Publishing Company

Name: ______________________________ Date: ______________

Activity 8J

# Step 3H: More Preliminary Research

**Directions:** Please use the following information to guide you as you take notes.

## Taking Notes

**A.** Do not let taking notes intimidate you. Let's start with the basics. What is a notecard? A notecard is simply a 3″x 5″ index card on which you write information from your sources. Notecards contain the information that you might include in your written or oral research report. There are also electronic versions of note cards that you could use or create.

**B.** There are four basic kinds of notecards to consider when doing research:

- *Source Cards*

Your actual NOTECARDS with notes could be:

- *Quotation Cards*
- *Paraphrase Cards*
- *Summary or Combination Cards*

## SOURCE CARDS—The first type of cards:

A SOURCE CARD is a card that has an MLA source citation written on the card. You will use these actual sources to write "notecards" on your topic.

When you begin working on your research, you will go to a variety of sources for information. Each time you begin working with a new source, you should complete a source card.

Copyright © Kendall Hunt Publishing Company

**8J** **Step 3H: More Preliminary Research (Continued)**

**On each card you will record:**

1. All the publication information required to include this source in your Works Cited list.
2. In the upper right hand corner, a code letter that you will use on all notecards that come from this source. (See the example notecard.)
3. The call number of the book or website's address, the URL, so you can locate it later.

***Example of a Source Note Card.*** *Some students find color coding their sources helpful.*

| **SOURCE A** |
|---|
| **Author(s):** |
| **Title:** |
| **City and state of publication:** |
| **Publishing company:** |
| **Copyright date:** |
| **Date found:** |

Copyright © Kendall Hunt Publishing Company

You will make a SOURCE CARD for each source you read, look at, or examine:

- *Books*
- *Magazines, Newspapers*
- *Reference Materials*
- *Websites*
- *Tracts, Pamphlets*
- *Interviews, etc.*

The part that causes most people to cringe is discarding a source that proves not to be useful after all. At some point, you may decide that the source just isn't truly useful for your research, or you may determine that you will not need to use that source. As painful as it may feel at first, disposing of something you took your time to read and record is part of every research project. You may question why you wouldn't only make a source card when you are sure you're going to use the resource, but you will save yourself time and trouble in the long run by learning how to do this step, knowing you have the ability to choose your evidence wisely and carefully. Get in the habit of doing a source card before you do anything else with a resource.

**Two examples of Source Cards:**

***Example of a Source Note Card for a Book:***

**SOURCE A**

**Author(s):** Stephen L. Harris and Gloria Platner

**Title:** *Classical Mythology: Images and Insights, $4^{th}$ Edition*

**City and state of publication:** Burr Ridge, IL

**Publishing company:** McGraw-Hill

**Copyright date:** 2003

**Date found:** November 30, 2014

Copyright © Kendall Hunt Publishing Company

8J Step 3H: More Preliminary Research (Continued)

*Example of a Source Note Card for a Web Site:*

**SOURCE B**

**Author(s):** Scholastic, Inc. editors

**Title:** *Immigration: Stories of Yesterday and Today "Three Recent Immigrants"*

**City and state of publication:**

**Publishing company:** Scholastic, Inc.

**Web address:** http://teacher.scholastic.com/activities/immigration/recent/answer.htm

**Copyright date:** 2011

**Date found:** November 25, 2014

**The actual NOTECARDS with evidence you will use.**

**Quotation Cards:**

You will use Quotation notecards to record a word-for-word quote from its source. Take care that you have all the information you need.

- *Always include the writer/author of the quote*
- *Punctuate correctly with quotation marks*
- *Only use direct quotations for very important passages*
- *Don't copy ANY sentences from a source without showing that you are using a direct quotation.*

Copyright © Kendall Hunt Publishing Company

## Step 3H: More Preliminary Research (Continued)

| | |
|---|---|
| **QUOTE** | **A**<br>**Page 16** |

Contributions of Augustus

"Because of Augustus and the stable form of government he created, Rome was able to survive for centuries more."

Kathryn Hinds

### Paraphrase Cards:

Paraphrase cards are used to record information, from the source, in your own words after you have read, considered the information, and thought of how you would tell this information to someone else.

- Write in complete sentences, in your style—this allows you to avoid plagiarism
- Write in your vocabulary, not the author's
- Write your understanding of the ideas—even add ideas that you may need to research further

| | |
|---|---|
| **PARAPHRASE** | **A**<br>**Page 16** |

Contributions of Augustus

Augustus helped the government of Rome to be stable, and so due to his leadership, the empire lasted for several centuries.

There were other reasons that it lasted. Augustus conquered a lot of land, and more people had enough to live well so they were more content.

Copyright © Kendall Hunt Publishing Company

**Combination Cards:**

Combination cards are used to summarize information or opinions in the resource you have read and considered.

- May contain a short quote to support a summary
- May include the source of the quote, if used or given
- May be useful in drawing conclusions or making observations as you present your research

| | |
|---|---|
| | A |
| **COMBINATION** | **Page 12** |

Changes under Constantine

Two major changes that occurred during the reign of Constantine:

1. Constantinople became the capital of the area.
2. Christianity became the religion.

These changes "marked a break with the past, although the Roman Empire continued to survive for roughly another 150 years."

Consider how Constantine changed the world not just during his lifetime, but for generations after, too.

Copyright © Kendall Hunt Publishing Company

**An Important Note about Notes:**

A note card should contain information about only one piece of information. Give each note a distinct title. Though this is tough, do not use the same title on any two cards, but **use similar titles for notes on the same topic.** Good titles on your cards will pay off greatly when you begin to sort them out! When you're ready to organize (or make an outline), you simply try out the order of the titles to see what works or flows best. The beauty of physical notecards is the ability to manipulate them on the desktop in order to find the best organization for your particular topic and the points you are striving to make.

**All Note Cards Should Have These Items:**

1. **Label:** Put this in the upper left hand corner. This label clearly describes the information in the note.

2. **Source Code:** Put this identifier in the upper right hand corner. This code comes from the source card and is used to identify the source of the note. Using a letter designator for each source just makes this easier when you organize your Works Cited or Bibliography and any internal citations. By following this method, your Works Cited almost writes itself!

3. **Specific Page Number:** Put this page number(s) next to the source code or just underneath it. This reminds you of the specific page from which you took the note, making citations much easier. In addition, if you read the note and decide you need a bit more information, you can easily go back to that source in the exact spot where the facts were given.

4. **Notes:** This is the actual information you gain from the source.

Copyright © Kendall Hunt Publishing Company

Name: ______________________________ Date: ______________

## Step 4A: Burning Question

**Directions:** Use the following information to help you develop your burning questions about your issue.

You have narrowed down your issue somewhat. You have gathered sources, read them, written source cards and notecards, and have a great deal of the work completed. Now that you have collected information about your issue, consider why or how you wish to develop an argument and persuade others. That *why* or *how* is immensely important. Decide how you can form a question that guides your understanding now that you have a better knowledge base. You may want to try two or three to see which best fits your ideas. Think of this as your Burning Question, the question that drives you to find your own answer to it and to want to develop an argument and persuade others to think as you do or to take action in a certain way.

**Student A Examples:**

*How does a dictatorship work better than a republic?*

*Why does a strong military presence allow economic growth?*

*How are ancient military strategies guiding today's military?*

**Student B Examples:**

*How do immigrants benefit our city?*

*Why do so many immigrants have service industry jobs?*

*How could our city assist recent immigrants? Why should we?*

**Burning Questions**

______________________________________________

______________________________________________

______________________________________________

Copyright © Kendall Hunt Publishing Company

Name: ______________________ Date: ______________

# Activity 8L

## Step 4B: Thesis

**Directions:** Use the following information to help to develop your thesis.

### Thesis

Looking at your burning question(s), what is a strong statement that puts forth how you feel about your main idea for your paper?

### Student A Examples:

*Today's military examines historic battles, famous leaders, and the latest technology to continue their mission.*

*A strong military provides economic growth for supply industries, jobs for the volunteers, and improved morale for the nation.*

### Student B Examples:

*Immigrants provide workers for entry-level and service-industry positions that are abundant in the city.*

*The cultural enrichment, the willingness to take jobs in the service industry, and the community development that immigrants bring to a city are significant reasons to welcome these groups and individuals.*

Your thesis is one sentence that will guide your entire paper. This statement should be a clear beacon to anyone reading or hearing your paper on what to expect. Try to write your thesis draft. Remember, you may want to polish and revise it along the way, but it should be the overall roadmap that points to the rest of your piece. Notice that it states a strong position that is debatable and that it mentions the points that support that view.

Copyright © Kendall Hunt Publishing Company

8L Step 4B: Thesis (Continued)

## Thesis Drafts

## Revised and More Polished Thesis

## Polished Thesis

Copyright © Kendall Hunt Publishing Company

Name: ______________________________ Date: ______________

# Step 5A: Examining Your Information

**Activity 9A**

Now that you have collected information on your topic and written a solid thesis, it is time to organize that information so that it can be the most useful to you.

## Sorting and Grouping

Go through your note cards and divide them into general categories. For example, if your topic is the U.S. military, you may find that you have collected notes on the following related topics: recruitment, battles, leadership, weapons, training, the branches of the military, and famous military leaders. Consider your own notecards and what information you have gathered. Place your cards on the desktop or table. Examine your thesis again. Sort your cards into the categories that relate to your thesis and substantiate your opinion.

Write your working thesis:

______________________________________________

______________________________________________

Now, sort your note cards into general categories. If you are not satisfied with the way you've sorted the cards, look at your thesis once more, and sort the cards into other categories. Now list the categories:

1. ______________________________
2. ______________________________
3. ______________________________
4. ______________________________
5. ______________________________

Copyright © Kendall Hunt Publishing Company

## Step 5A: Examining Your Information (Continued)

You may find some cards with interesting facts that just don't fit into any of your categories. You may wish to keep these cards in a category that you designate as "extra" for the time being, but remember, it is okay to discard some notecards if you find they do not provide needed evidence.

### Evaluating the Information

Review your categories. Which have the most notes and solid evidence? Put a circle around the number of those top 3–4 categories that you generated above.

Now, examine which category or categories have the least information. Put an X over the number of those one to two categories that do not seem as strong as the others.

Next, the tough part. Have you found enough information to support your ideas? Did you find answers for all of your original questions?

If you think you still haven't completely supported your ideas or do not have answers to your questions, what information do you still need?

A. ______________________________

B. ______________________________

C. ______________________________

This is the time to do additional research if you need more information.

Copyright © Kendall Hunt Publishing Company

Name: ______________________________ Date: ______________

# Step 5B: Outlining Your Information

At some point you've seen or written an outline. You are going to do a traditional outline, but you can choose whether to do a simple phrase outline or a sentence outline. (Choose one style. Do not mix them.) Keep the following guidelines in mind when writing your outline:

1. Put your thesis statement at the top.
2. Make ideas parallel.
3. Use a clear sentence or phrase for each point.
4. You are to create a standard outline. Remember, you must have at least two points in a sub-area. You should have at least three main points or categories that support your thesis. Try to limit the number of sections (think large Roman numerals) you designate.

Use the following system of numbers and letters:

Thesis: ______________________________

**I.** ______________________________

**A.** ______________________________

**B.** ______________________________

**1.** ______________________________

**2.** ______________________________

**a.** ______________________________

**b.** ______________________________

Copyright © Kendall Hunt Publishing Company

## 9B Step 5B: Outlining Your Information (Continued)

II. ______________________________

A. ______________________________

B. ______________________________

III. ______________________________

A. ______________________________

1. ______________________________

2. ______________________________

B. ______________________________

As you prepare to write, you may need to revise your outline. Remember to be flexible and willing to change your outline if necessary.

Try to draft your own outline now.

Copyright © Kendall Hunt Publishing Company

Name: ______________________________ Date: ______________

# Steps 6–10: More Research, Check It Out, and First Draft Review, Revise, Edit, and Publish

Go for a walk, play basketball, do a race on your Wii, get a drink of water, make a Vine and post it, text a friend, climb a tree, weed the garden, write in your notebook, make dinner for your family, bathe the dog, ride your bike. In other words, step away from what you've done for just a bit so that when you look it over again, you are able to see it with clarity.

**Step 6: More Research**

Look over your Thesis and Outline. Are there any gaps that you need to fill? If so, go get more information.

**Step 7: Check It Out**

Go ahead and start your Works Cited page. This allows you to see that you have everything in MLA format, and it will enable you to easily insert your internal citations as you write. If you have a text or site that you are uncertain about how to format the citation, ask for help.

***To Write Your Works Cited Page:*** You are going to center the words Works Cited at the top of the page, then list all the sources used in your paper, in alphabetical order, by the author's last name. Following the author's last name, list the information you wrote on your Source Card. Who, What, Where, When is a good way to remember the order in which to put this information.

The Purdue Online Writing Lab at http://owl.english.purdue.edu/owl/resource/747/12/ has updated examples of a Works Cited page to look at as a model.

Copyright © Kendall Hunt Publishing Company

**9C** **Steps 6–10: More Research, Check it Out, and First Draft Review, Revise, Edit, and Publish (Continued)**

## Step 8: First Draft

Take a deep breath. You have done the difficult and time-consuming labor of your piece.

Now you write.

Never, ever turn in the first draft to your teacher. Do not hit the "print" button or hit "send" just because you are so happy and relieved to have completed a draft. Always give it a bit of "hibernation time" so that you can read it over with fresh eyes.

Remember, you must cite or document any information that is not your original idea. That's any time you use information from your notecards; that is why you made them. By making these, you've pulled out the ideas you found by researching. Now you will weave the evidence together with your understanding of the information to show the reader how you connected the evidence and reached your opinion.

***How to Do Internal Citations (sometimes called in-text documentation):*** As you write, you will put information about your sources directly into your paper whenever you use a direct quotation, statistics, paraphrase, etc. that you have from your notecards.

You must put an internal citation any time you use:

- a direct quote, whether a full quotation or phrase quote
- a summary of someone else's ideas
- a paraphrasing of an original idea

The Purdue Online Writing Lab at http://owl.english.purdue.edu/owl/resource/747/02/ has many examples of how internal citations appear.

Enjoy figuring out the best way to share the ideas you've found as you write. Allow your paper to reflect you and how you communicate.

Copyright © Kendall Hunt Publishing Company

## 9C Steps 6–10: More Research, Check it Out, and First Draft Review, Revise, Edit, and Publish (Continued)

### Step 9: Review, Revise, Edit

Try to consider how the ideas are formed, how the paper is organized, how words are used, how true to author's voice the project is, how fluent the sentences are, and how conventions are correctly used. Assessment is on-going as one writes, but having a Peer Review, Self-Evaluation, and Teacher Assessment pushes a writer to improve.

The number of drafts that you need may be more or less than other students. That's normal and okay! Just ask yourself, "Is this piece better than the one before?"

### Step 10: Publish

A Final Draft to be proud of has been completed if you have methodically followed these steps. You are a writer!

Copyright © Kendall Hunt Publishing Company

Name: ______________________________ Date: ______________

# Critical Thinking

Critical thinking can become a part of one's everyday life. Using Paul's Wheel of Reasoning can also help us understand other disciplines or pieces we encounter. Beyond literature and essays, reasoning can enable one to dig deeply into the layers of meanings in speeches, pieces of art, movies, music, and conversations. Read over the questions below and see which ones enable you to understand more deeply or analyze more fully, and then try to use those questions as you make notes in your Response Journal. Include any other observations or questions as you ponder and reexamine the piece carefully.

1. The individual felt it was important to create this piece (*article, art, music, short story, poem, book, research, speech, etc.*) because __________.

   **Purpose:** What is the purpose of this piece? What leads you to that reason?

2. The point of view with which this piece was created is __________.

   **Point of View:** What is the perspective of this piece? How consistent is the point of view? Are there other points of view involved?

3. The focus of this piece is __________.

   **Issue:** What is the central issue of this piece? What other issues are presented in this piece?

4. The most important information or evidence presented in this piece is __________.

   **Data/Evidence:** What evidence does the creator use to support her/his opinion? What evidence is presented that the central character is motivated by __________ (specific emotion)?

   What observations or facts are used to support the creator's conclusions?

Copyright © Kendall Hunt Publishing Company

## Critical Thinking (Continued)

5. Justice is __________ according to what the creator presents in this piece. My evidence or support for this is __________.

   **Assumptions:** What assumptions does the creator of this piece make about the concept of Justice? As you read/viewed/listened to this piece, what assumptions did you notice? Consider how the creator of this piece worked to dispel assumptions (perhaps those from another's perspective).

6. The creator of this piece may convince the audience to believe this line of reasoning, and the implications are __________.

   **Implications:** At this point in the piece, what are the implications of a character's behavior? Audience members may choose to act upon the reasoning the creator of this piece presents. What would be the consequences of such actions? If the protagonist does not change behavior, what are the implications? If the status quo continues, what are the implications?

7. Upon reflection, the creator implies certain beliefs. For the audience, the main inferences that can be drawn are __________.

   **Inferences:** What are the main conclusions the creator wants the audience to pull from this piece? Considering what has been presented (or has happened) thus far, what inferences can be drawn from the conclusion of this piece?

8. The creator has a "big idea" she/he wants the audience to see. The creator wants the audience to understand the central theme in this piece as __________.

   **Concept:** What was the overarching theme or main idea that the creator wanted audiences to understand when this piece was made? How do you know? What are the concepts of which one must be aware that add to the understanding of this piece? What do you know regarding the concepts this piece presents?

Copyright © Kendall Hunt Publishing Company

Name: ______________________________ Date: ______________

# Creative and Artistic Endeavors (A)

**Directions:**

1. Choose a song or piece of art from one of the sites below (or one you have found and sought approval for using).

2. Your time will be limited for choosing a piece, and you are to go to your teacher to have the choice recorded.

3. After you have your selection noted by your teacher, sit silently and look or listen (with headphones) to the piece. Use all of your senses as you observe or experience your selection.

4. Follow your teacher's instructions regarding how you will record your answers to the questions (Response Journal or electronically). Saying, "I like it" does not merit the term *analyze*, so dig deeply and do a bit of research if necessary.

5. Be ready to share your ideas with others when it is time.

**Sites with Songs and Art from or about the 1930s, 1940s, 1950s, or 1960s**

Library of Congress—site with posters from WPA
http://www.loc.gov/pictures/collection/wpapos/

Art in the 1960s—A wealth of images about the four art movements of the 1960s
http://www.artsconnected.org/collection/118487/art-in-the-1960s?print=true#%281%29

Paintings of the 1930s
http://en.wikipedia.org/wiki/Category:1930s_paintings

Paintings of the 1960s
http://en.wikipedia.org/wiki/Category:1960s_paintings

Copyright © Kendall Hunt Publishing Company

## 11B Creative and Artistic Endeavors (A) (Continued)

1930s Paintings
http://www.digplanet.com/wiki/Category:1930s_paintings

1960s Paintings
http://www.digplanet.com/wiki/Category:1960s_paintings

Library of Congress—site with songs from many eras
(keep focus on 1930s, 1940s, or 1960s)
http://www.loc.gov/teachers/classroommaterials/themes/america-music/exhibitions.html

Museum of Fine Arts Boston (1940s paintings)
http://www.mfa.org/search/collections?keyword=1940s&objecttype=54

Swing Out to Victory—Songs of WWII
http://www.allmusic.com/album/swing-out-to-victory-songs-of-wwii-mw0000603564

1960s Best Songs
http://www.boomerslife.org/best_songs_1960s_rock_and_roll_music_hits.htm

The '60s Top Ten Songs Chart
http://www.popculturemadness.com/Entertainment/Decades/60s/Music.html

VI Corps Proudly Presents the Music of WWII
http://www.6thcorpsmusic.us/index.html

Copyright © Kendall Hunt Publishing Company

Name: ______________________________ Date: ________________

# Creative and Artistic Endeavors (B)

## Questions to Consider

### For Art:

- From just looking at this painting, where do you think it takes place? When? What makes you think this?
- Who or what is the main focus in this piece? What is this character doing?
- From merely looking at the main focus, what two adjectives would you use to describe the person, animal, thing, etc.?
- Are there other points of focus that you are drawn to as you look at this piece?
- Who or what are the others in the painting? What are they doing? Is this a guess or is there something that lets you know this?
- What do you think happened before this painting was made that inspired the artist to create it?
- How do think the main subject feels?
- How do you feel when looking at this painting?
- What do you think this painting is called (if you haven't already seen the title)?
- What do you think the artist is saying about life or nature? Justice?

### For Songs:

- From just listening to this song, where and when does it take place? What makes you think this?
- Who or what is the main focus in this piece? What is this character doing (or experiencing)?
- What type of music is this piece, or how would you categorize it?
- Are there other points of focus that are part of this song?

Copyright © Kendall Hunt Publishing Company

- What is this song trying to tell people?
- What do you think happened before this song was created that inspired the artist?
- How do you feel when listening to this song?
- If you haven't yet done so, try to find the lyrics and read them. How does reading just the lyrics compare to listening to the song?
- What might you call this song if asked to retitle it?
- What do you think the artist is saying about life or nature? Relationships or communities? Justice?

**For All Types of Artistic Pieces:**

- Why were you drawn to this piece?
- What impacted your choice?
- What did you learn after talking with others about the piece?
- In what way does this selection illustrate justice or injustice?

Copyright © Kendall Hunt Publishing Company

Name: ______________________ Date: ____________

Activity 12A

# Literature Web

**Directions:** Complete a Literature Web for a chapter or section of your novel.

**Key Words**

**Feelings**

**Ideas**

**Title**

**Images/Symbols**

**Structure**

Copyright © Kendall Hunt Publishing Company

Name: ______________________________ Date: ______________

# Activity 12B

## Vocabulary Web

**Directions:** Complete a Vocabulary Web for a word from the vocabulary list for your novel.

**Word Families**

______________________
______________________
______________________
______________________
______________________
______________________
______________________

**Synonyms**

______________________
______________________

**Antonyms**

______________________
______________________

**Dictionary Definition**

______________________
______________________

**Word**

______________________

**Analysis**

**Part of Speech**

______________________

**Stems**

______________________
______________________
______________________
______________________

**Origin**

______________________
______________________
______________________

**Sentence in Text**

______________________
______________________
______________________
______________________

**Student Example**

______________________
______________________

Copyright © Kendall Hunt Publishing Company

Name: ______________________________ Date: ______________

# Vocabulary from *Of Mice and Men*

**Directions:** Review the vocabulary from the novel as directed by your teacher.

1. aloof
2. apprehension
3. belligerent
4. bindle
5. cesspool
6. contemplate
7. crestfallen
8. derision
9. derogatory
10. drone
11. fawning
12. indignation
13. liniment
14. maul
15. mollify
16. monotonous
17. morose
18. mottled
19. ominous
20. pantomime
21. pugnacious
22. receptive
23. recumbent
24. reprehensible
25. reverence
26. reverently
27. rheumatism
28. woe
29. writhe

Copyright © Kendall Hunt Publishing Company

Name: ______________________________ Date: ______________

# Vocabulary from *No Promises in the Wind*

**Directions:** Review the vocabulary from the novel as directed by your teacher.

1. ballyhoo
2. begrudged
3. brusque
4. callous
5. capricious
6. complacent
7. convalescence
8. decrepit
9. desolation
10. docile
11. imperceptible
12. improvident
13. improvisation
14. incredulously
15. indifferent
16. ingenuity
17. listless
18. loll
19. nonchalant
20. paltry
21. patronizing
22. pompous
23. ramshackle
24. rancor
25. ravine
26. resonant
27. sallow
28. sober
29. toil
30. tottered

Copyright © Kendall Hunt Publishing Company

Name: ______________________________ Date: ______________

# Novel Assessment Choices

You may choose one of the following assessments. All of these choices should focus on social justice. The concept of social justice involves a balance between an individual's responsibility and society's joint responsibilities to contribute to a just society. Consider how the novel you read exemplifies the generalizations about justice.

Your assignment should include a meaningful title, cited references (from the book), and your name. It should be in publishable form.

Choose ONE of the following:

1. **Character Analysis**

   Choose a character from your novel. Consider the ways that characterization makes an impression. Characterization includes what a character says, does, and others say about him/her. Indicate how the character is impacted by social justice or injustice. Use at least three textual references to support your ideas, citing the source MLA style. (*1–2 pages total, typed, double-spaced.*)

2. **Cartoon Strip**

   Create a five- to ten-frame cartoon strip that captures a scene of social justice or injustice. Find two to three direct parts or quotes from the book to reference. Choose a scene that captures a powerful moment that made an impression on you. (*In ink. Unlined paper. Minimum one page with five to ten panels. Dialogue or captions with at least two citations.*)

Copyright © Kendall Hunt Publishing Company

### 3. Artistic Rendering, Mobile, or Collage

Create a piece of art, a mobile, or a collage that captures one important aspect of the story. This should be tied to social justice or injustice. For each item, you need to write an explanation and citation. Be sure to explain why you chose it, what it represents, and how it ties to social justice or injustice. Include citations from the book. (*Art or collage should be on unlined paper or canvas of at least 8½ by 11 inches. A mobile should be at least 11 by 17 inches. All pieces should be presentation-ready.*)

### 4. Poem or Song

Consider how your novel's events, setting, and characters tie to social justice or injustice. Write a poem or song characterizing an aspect of social justice or injustice in the story. Include citations at the bottom or on another page. Make sure when you write it, that the appearance is that of a poem or a song, written in stanzas, and possibly with a chorus.

### 5. Character Dialogue

Write a dialogue between one of the characters from *Of Mice and Men* or *No Promises in the Wind* and Abraham Lincoln or Lucy Stone as if they were traveling together. What might they talk about? Where might they go? Would they get along or argue? Who would drive? How does each think regarding social justice and injustice? Show these details through the dialogue you create. Be specific with citations from the novel. Be creative! (*Create a minimum of 1½ pages of dialogue. Typed. Double-spaced.*)

Copyright © Kendall Hunt Publishing Company

Name: ________________________________ Date: ________________

# Selected Quotes on Justice and Quotes from *To Kill a Mockingbird* and *Warriors Don't Cry*

**Activity 15A**

**Directions:** Follow your teacher's instructions to identify the parts of speech in the following quotations.

"Her voice didn't sound frightened, but I could feel her hand shaking and the perspiration in her palm."

**From *Warriors Don't Cry* Ch. 11**

"He said he gave us credit when we didn't have eating money, so he expected us to pay without complaining."

**From *Warriors Don't Cry* Ch. 7**

"Three weeks later, having won a federal court order, we black children maneuvered our way past an angry mob …"

**From *Warriors Don't Cry* Ch. 5**

"Maycomb was an old town, but it was a tired, old town when I first knew it."

**From *To Kill a Mockingbird* Ch. 1**

"Bad language is a stage all children go through, and it dies with time when they learn they're not attracting attention with it."

**From *To Kill a Mockingbird* Ch. 7**

Copyright © Kendall Hunt Publishing Company

**15A** **Selected Quotes on Justice and Quotes from *To Kill a Mockingbird* and *Warriors Don't Cry* (Continued)**

"The virtue of justice consists in moderation, as regulated by wisdom."

**—Aristotle**

"Justice consists not in being neutral between right and wrong, but in finding out the right and upholding it, wherever found, against the wrong."

**—Theodore Roosevelt**

"Injustice anywhere is a threat to justice everywhere."

**—Martin Luther King Jr.**

Copyright © Kendall Hunt Publishing Company

Name: ______________________ Date: ______________

# Vocabulary from *To Kill a Mockingbird*

**Directions:** Review the vocabulary from the novel as directed by your teacher.

1. acquiescence
2. arid
3. assuage
4. auspicious
5. beadle
6. blandly
7. bovine
8. changelings
9. church
10. collards
11. connived
12. contentious
13. covey
14. crepey
15. deportment
16. dictum
17. doused
18. entailment
19. expunge
20. façade
21. fey
22. furtive
23. gait
24. heathen
25. hookahs
26. illicitly
27. impudent
28. ingenuous
29. invective
30. iota
31. irascible
32. jarred
33. lavations
34. mollified
35. myopic
36. obstreperous

Copyright © Kendall Hunt Publishing Company

## 15B Vocabulary from *To Kill a Mockingbird* (Continued)

37. passé
38. predilection
39. prowess
40. quelling
41. recluse
42. remorse
43. riled
44. rout
45. scrip stamps
46. shinny
47. smilax
48. snuff
49. statute
50. sundry
51. taut
52. temerity
53. tenet
54. tight
55. touchous
56. trousseau
57. venerable
58. wallowing
59. wary

Copyright © Kendall Hunt Publishing Company

Name: ______________________________ Date: ________________

# Vocabulary from *Warriors Don't Cry*

**Directions:** Review the vocabulary from the novel as directed by your teacher.

1. accolades
2. adamant
3. anteroom
4. barrage
5. belligerent
6. chide
7. copious
8. deity
9. dither
10. edict
11. effigy
12. emaciated
13. enclave
14. fiasco
15. fracas
16. frivolity
17. gauntlet
18. impasse
19. impeccably
20. insolent
21. kowtow
22. livid
23. melee
24. moot
25. nonchalant
26. ominous
27. ostracized
28. placating
29. pristine
30. proviso
31. quash
32. respite
33. reverberate
34. tarry
35. tenacious
36. tolerable

Copyright © Kendall Hunt Publishing Company

## 15C Vocabulary from *Warriors Don't Cry* (Continued)

**37.** trounced

**38.** unmitigated

**39.** veneer

**40.** vicarious

Copyright © Kendall Hunt Publishing Company

Name: ______________________________ Date: ______________

Activity 15D

# Vocabulary Web

**Directions:** Complete a Vocabulary Web for the selected word from your novel.

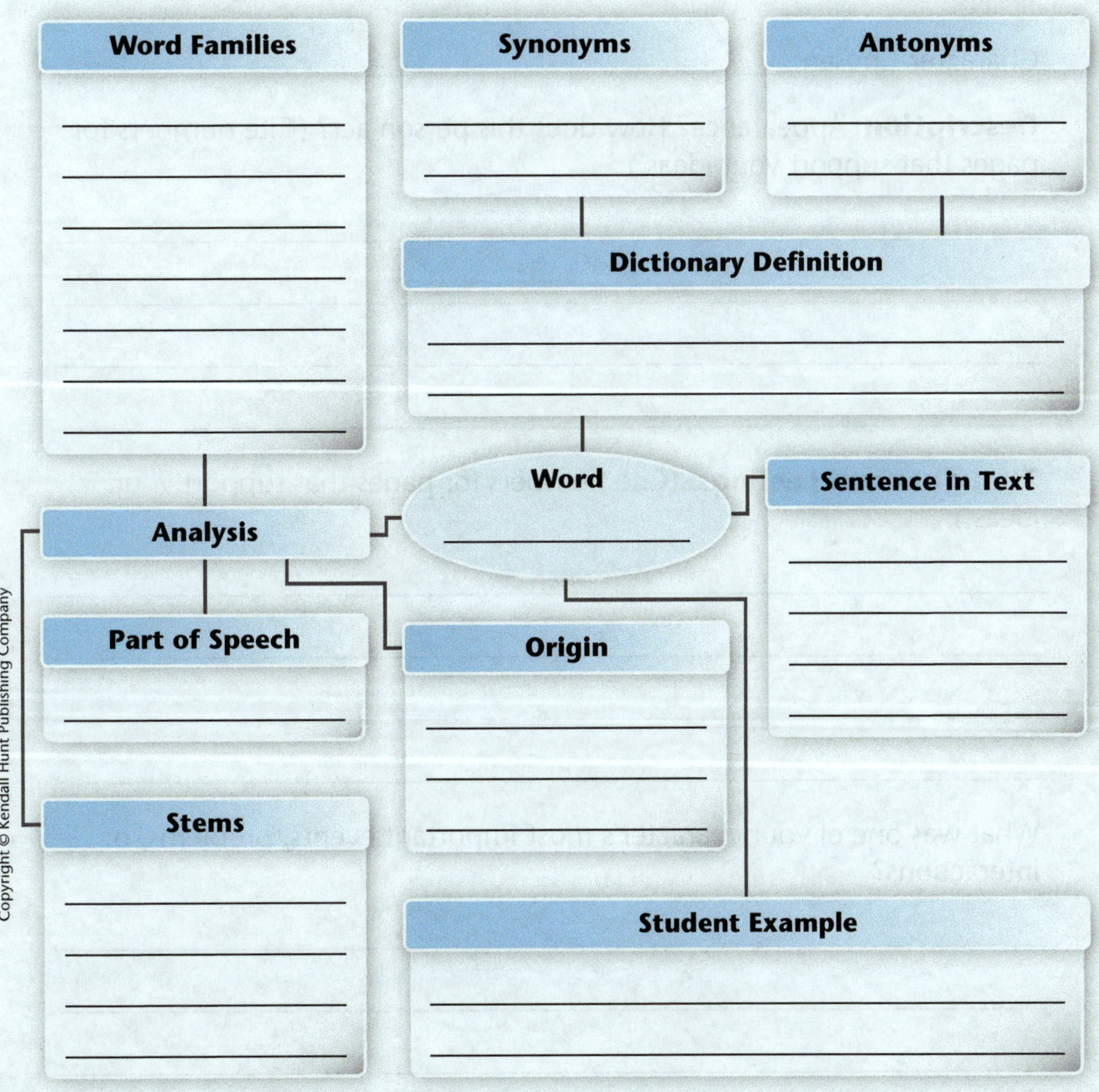


Copyright © Kendall Hunt Publishing Company

Name: ______________________ Date: ____________

Activity 15E

# Close Examination of a Character

Think of how characters in books are analyzed based upon appearance, what they say, what they do, what others say about them, and their thoughts.

Character Chosen ______________________

**Description:** Appearance? How does this person act? (Cite numbers for pages that support your ideas.):

______________________

______________________

______________________

______________________

**Thoughts and Feelings:** (Cite numbers for pages that support your ideas.):

______________________

______________________

______________________

______________________

What was one of your character's most important events, problems, or interactions?

______________________

______________________

______________________

______________________

Copyright © Kendall Hunt Publishing Company

**15E** **Close Examination of a Character (Continued)**

What are two things your character says that caught your attention? (Cite page numbers for your quotes.)

____________________________________________________________

____________________________________________________________

____________________________________________________________

____________________________________________________________

What would your character's symbol be? Explain.

____________________________________________________________

____________________________________________________________

____________________________________________________________

____________________________________________________________

Using this information, consider the importance of symbols and images. Examine what you found upon analyzing this character. Create a coat of arms, a family crest, or a family flag that weaves together what you found. You must use at least one of the quotes of importance that your character said. Do not identify who the character is on the front of the flag or coat of arms; place citations on the reverse side, as well as your name(s). Your project may be created using drawings or found images. It must be at least 8½ by 11 inches in size on unlined paper. For further help in creating this piece, you may wish to use the following sites:

To see meanings of symbols:

Dictionary of Symbolism http://www.umich.edu/~umfandsf/symbolismproject/symbolism.html/

To see meanings of colors:

http://changingminds.org/disciplines/communication/color_effect.htm

Copyright © Kendall Hunt Publishing Company

## 15E Close Examination of a Character (Continued)

To see examples of coats of arms:

http://www.makeyourcoatofarms.com/

http://www.heraldry.ws/

http://www.fleurdelis.com/meanings.htm

http://www.familynamecoatofarms.com/

To see examples of family crests and flags:

http://www.coatofarms.com/family-crest-flags-banners.html

http://www.mytribe101.com/crest/

Copyright © Kendall Hunt Publishing Company

Name: ______________________________ Date: ______________

Activity 16A

# Literature Web

**Directions:** Complete a Literature Web for a chapter or section of your novel.

**Key Words**

**Feelings**

**Ideas**

**Title**

**Images/Symbols**

**Structure**

Copyright © Kendall Hunt Publishing Company

Name: ______________________________ Date: ______________

Activity 16B

# Building Meaning Through Multi-Genre Reflection: *To Kill a Mockingbird* & *Warriors Don't Cry*

Let's explore a project that hits on multiple intelligences and multiple levels of literacies for our books *To Kill a Mockingbird* or *Warriors Don't Cry*. You will be required to complete ONE of the projects listed. Read each description carefully and then choose the one you can complete the BEST to showcase your knowledge and skills. You will be graded on how you demonstrate a connection to the book, creativity, your analysis of the book, completeness, and product excellence.

A. Write an **Original Song** to represent the novel—Pick three or four of the main events or points that you think would be the best ones to carry forth the ideas and characters within the book. Write song lyrics and music. Be sure to give it a meaningful title. Also, design the CD cover and liner notes; the cover and liner notes can be larger than a CD's case. You have the option to "burn" the CD you designed and turn it in (clearly labeled), perform the song live (and turn in lyrics and your cover design), or film yourself (making the film available and turning in lyrics and your cover design).

B. Design a **Quilt** that shows three or four of the main events from the book. Create at least five unique squares or pieces that tell your analysis of the book. Think of characters, events, symbols, etc. Design the quilt pieces (at least eight by eight inches, made of paper or fabric) and on the back write an explanation of what that quilt square represents, using textual evidence. (If you really know how to sew, you could make an apron that represents the book.)

Copyright © Kendall Hunt Publishing Company

**16B** **Building Meaning Through Multi-Genre Reflection:** ***To Kill a Mockingbird*** **&** ***Warriors Don't Cry*** **(Continued)**

C. **Artistic License**—Create a piece of artwork that represents the major themes (be sure to include justice!), characters, conflicts, symbols, and plot in the novel. You may do a painting or some other drawing (collage). NOTE: DO NOT attempt this if you do not like to draw or paint. Turn in the piece of artwork and a typewritten one- to three-paragraph analysis with textual evidence that explains how it represents the novel. Be creative in your use of medium/genre (paints, pastels, pointillism, abstract, collaging, etc).

D. **Graphic Novel**—Choose a short, powerful scene that you enjoyed in the book. Create a graphic novel of this scene that has at least twelve panels with both visual elements and dialogue. These panels do not all have to fit on one page—in fact, do not put more than six panels maximum on one sheet of paper! Plan your scenes out in pencil first. Near the top of the first page, you should put the title of the scene and a narrative box that tells the book title and pages referenced. Be sure your finished piece is neatly colored in or inked on unlined paper at least 8½ by 11 inches in size. In one to three typed paragraphs on a separate sheet of paper, explain why you chose to represent the scene in the manner you did. The quality of your project will be determined by how well you executed the scene and explained your choices.

E. Create a **Museum** or **Theme Park**—Design a museum or theme park about the book. You should design and name at least five exhibits or rides/attractions. You may include shows as well. The overall park itself should reflect the major aspects of the book. You need to create a detailed drawing, map, or 3D model of your creation with all parts labeled. You may not merely use a program or application that allows you to create an amusement park, nor should you go to a hobby store and merely purchase small-scale miniature items to place on a board or foam core. In addition, you have to type a one- to three-paragraph explanation (with textual evidence) that explains why you chose what you did and how you think it fits the book. Keep in mind scale, tie-ins to the novel, and the textual evidence.

Copyright © Kendall Hunt Publishing Company

## 16B Building Meaning Through Multi-Genre Reflection: *To Kill a Mockingbird* & *Warriors Don't Cry* (Continued)

F. Keeping a **Journal** or **Letter Writing**—Pretend you are one of the characters (other than Scout or Melba, since we already know about them). You are keeping a journal of some of the major events that occur in the novel in which you are involved. Turn in the pieces (either four journal entries or a total of four letters) with a brief typed explanation (one to three paragraphs) of why you chose that character. Include supporting details from the book. (This could also be a "scrapbook" journal.)

G. **Creative U**—Have a great idea? See your teacher for approval. Demonstrate that your idea will show greater depth of understanding and create connections that you wish to explore further.

Copyright © Kendall Hunt Publishing Company

Name: ______________________ Date: ______________

Activity 17A

# Standards of Reasoning

Evaluate the issues of Indian Boarding Schools that you read and viewed. Respond to the following questions, keeping in mind the time frame of each piece.

1. **Clarity.** Were the reasons for creating the Indian schools clear? Were they explained thoroughly, or was more information needed? How might the writings be clearer?

______________________________________________

______________________________________________

______________________________________________

______________________________________________

2. **Accuracy.** Is the supporting evidence accurate and correct? What improvements could have been made?

______________________________________________

______________________________________________

______________________________________________

______________________________________________

3. **Precision.** Were the reasons and evidence specific? Were the reasons general and vague? What improvements could have been made?

______________________________________________

______________________________________________

______________________________________________

______________________________________________

Copyright © Kendall Hunt Publishing Company

Name: ______________________________ Date: ______________

Activity 18A

# Vocabulary from *The Night Thoreau Spent in Jail*

**Directions:** Review the vocabulary from the novel as directed by your teacher.

1. abet
2. alacrity
3. conformity
4. dilemma
5. esteem
6. ethics
7. euphemism
8. expedient
9. fain
10. leaven
11. magnanimity
12. manipulate
13. motive
14. novel
15. perverted
16. posse comitatus
17. posterity
18. strait
19. sublime
20. superfluous
21. transcendentalism

Copyright © Kendall Hunt Publishing Company

Name: ______________________ Date: ____________

# Activity 18B

## Vocabulary Web

**Directions:** Complete a Vocabulary Web for a word from the list for "The Night Thoreau Spent in Jail."

**Word Families**

**Synonyms**

**Antonyms**

**Dictionary Definition**

**Word**

**Sentence in Text**

**Analysis**

**Part of Speech**

**Origin**

**Stems**

**Student Example**

Copyright © Kendall Hunt Publishing Company

Name: ______________________ Date: ______________

Activity 18C

# Literature Web

**Directions:** Complete a Literature Web for an act from "The Night Thoreau Spent in Jail."

**Key Words**

**Feelings**

**Ideas**

**Title**

**Images/Symbols**

**Structure**

Copyright © Kendall Hunt Publishing Company

Name: ______________________ Date: __________



# Language Arts Reflection

What is The Pursuit of Justice?

________________________________

________________________________

How did you grow as a reader during this unit? As a writer? As a communicator? As a researcher?

*Reader:* ________________________________

________________________________

*Writer:* ________________________________

________________________________

*Communicator:* ________________________________

________________________________

*Researcher:* ________________________________

________________________________

What selection was your favorite and why?

________________________________

________________________________

What selection was one that you do not think should be in the unit and why?

________________________________

________________________________

Copyright © Kendall Hunt Publishing Company

## 20A Language Arts Reflection (Continued)

What selection do you think should be added to this unit?

_______________________________________________

_______________________________________________

What was the most challenging aspect of this unit? Explain.

_______________________________________________

_______________________________________________

Which of your skills need further polishing?

_______________________________________________

_______________________________________________

Which of your skills grew the most?

_______________________________________________

_______________________________________________

Please share this information with your parents and ask one of them to sign below.

| ______________________ | ______________________ |
|---|---|
| Student Signature | Parent Signature |

Copyright © Kendall Hunt Publishing Company

Name: ______________________ Date: ______________

Activity 20B

# Literature Web

**Directions:** Complete a Literature Web for "Another April."

**Key Words**

**Feelings**

**Ideas**

**Title**

**Images/Symbols**

**Structure**

Copyright © Kendall Hunt Publishing Company

CPSIA information can be obtained
at www.ICGtesting.com
Printed in the USA
LVHW05s1157090518
576531LV00002B/4/P